EXPLORING
BORDER REIVERS
HISTORY

EXPLORING
BORDER REIVERS
HISTORY

PHILIP NIXON ARPS. LMPA. DipPP

breedon **books**
PUBLISHING

First published in Great Britain in 2007 by

The Breedon Books Publishing Company Limited

Breedon House, 3 The Parker Centre, Derby, DE21 4SZ.

ISBN 978-1-85983-583-8

Printed and bound by Butler and Tanner, Frome, Somerset

Contents

Acknowledgements 8

Introduction 9

The Border Reivers 11

Rise of the Reiver 12

    Robert the Bruce 17

Border Marches 18

    Drumlanrig Tower, Hawick 19

    Eildon Hills 20

    Old Border Gaol, Hexham 21

    Larriston Fell 25

    March Wardens 26

    Redheuch – Liddesdale 28

    The Hot Trod 29

    Days of Truce 30

    The Reivers and their way of life 33

    Upper Denton, near Gilsland 35

    Reiver Names and Nicknames or To-names 38

    The Tools of Reiving 39

    The Market Cross, Ancrum 40

    The Capon Tree – Jedburgh 41

    Reiving and Raiding 42

    Reiver presentation – Tullie House Museum 42

    The Muckle Toon Bell – Carlisle 43

    Theeves Roads 44

    Plaque – Carlisle Castle 47

    Ponteland pele tower 50

    The Union of the Crowns 50

The Riding Families 52

Border History 53

    Alnwick Castle, Northumberland 53

    Arthuret Church, Longtown 56

    Askerton Castle, Gilsland 58

    Aydon Castle, Corbridge 60

    The Battle of Ancrum Moor – 12 February 1534 66

The Battle of Flodden Field 68

The Battle of Halidon Hill 71

The Battle of Otterburn 73

Berwick-upon-Tweed 76

Bewcastle, Cumbria 82

Black Middens Bastle, near Bellingham, Northumberland 84

Brackenhill Tower, Longtown 87

St Michael's Church, Burgh-by-Sands 88

Caerlaverock Castle, Dumfries 89

Carlisle Castle 92

Carlisle Cathedral 95

Cartington Castle, Rothbury 96

Cessford Castle, Morebattle 97

Dally Castle, near Bellingham, Northumberland 98

The Devil's Beeftub — Moffat 99

Dryburgh Abbey, Melrose 102

Edward I Monument — Burgh-by-Sands 105

Etal Castle, Northumberland 107

Ferniehirst Castle, Jedburgh 109

The Fish Garth and Coop House on the River Esk, near Canonbie 111

Ford Castle, Northumberland 114

Galloway Nagges or Reiver Horses 116

Greenknowe Tower, Gordon 117

Harbottle Castle, Northumberland 120

Hermitage Castle, Liddesdale 121

Home Castle, Roxburghshire 125

Housesteads Bastle House 126

Jedburgh Abbey 127

Jock o' the Side's Escape From Newcastle 128

Johnnie Armstrong of Gilnockie 129

Kelso Abbey 132

Kinmont Willie 134

Kirkhope Tower, Ettrickbridge 137

Lanercost Priory, Brampton 140

Langholm Castle 142

Liddel Castle, near Newcastleton 143

Lochmaben Castle 144

Low Cleughs Bastle, near West Woodburn, Northumberland 145

Mangerton Tower, Liddesdale 146

Mary, Queen of Scots House, Jedburgh 148

Melrose Abbey 149

Muckle Mouthed Meg 150

Naworth Castle, Brampton 151

Neidpath Castle, Peebles 153

Newcastleton and Liddesdale 154

Norham Castle 156

Otterburn Tower, Otterburn 158

Preston Tower, Northumberland 159

The Redeswire Fray – 7 July 1575 160

Repentance Tower, Ecclefechan, Dumfries and Galloway 162

Roxburgh Castle, near Kelso 162

Shittleheugh Bastle House, Otterburn 164

Slewe Dogges 166

Smailholm Tower 166

St Cuthbert's Church, Bellingham, Northumberland 168

St Cuthbert's Church, Corsenside 169

St John's Church, Newton Arlosh, Cumbria .169

Tarras Moss 170

Tarset Castle, Northumberland 172

The Battle of Dryfe Sands, Lockerbie – 6 December 1593 172

The Battle of Solway Moss – 24 November 1542 175

The Bishop's Curse, the Cursing Stone, Carlisle 177

The Debatable Land and the Scots Dike 179

The Lochmabenstane, Old Graitney, Gretna .181

The Sieur de la Bastie, Warden of the Scottish East March 181

Thirlwall Castle 182

Threave Castle, Castle Douglas 184

Torthorwald Castle, Torthorwald, Dumfries .186

Tosson Tower, Rothbury 187

Triermain Castle, near Brampton, Cumbria 188

Warkworth Castle 189

Woodhouses Bastle, near Rothbury, Northumberland 190

The Border Ballads 191

Acknowledgements

Thanks to everyone at Breedon Books for their encouragement, enthusiasm, and, of course, giving me the opportunity, especially Steve Caron, Michelle Grainger and Matt Limbert.

Much appreciation for the great help given by my good friends John Humphries, John Stephenson, Denis Dunlop, Hugh Dias and Dorothy Chadwick.

Thanks also to English Heritage, the Dean and Chapter of Carlisle Cathedral, Tullie House Museum, Hexham Border Gaol and all those individuals who contributed with comment, information and advice.

Many thanks and much appreciation to my family, Val, Mark, Sophy and Archie the Labrador for their unfailing support and living on a diet of information on everything 'reiver' for the past two years as well as their company on far flung expeditions throughout the region in the relentless pursuit of research and photography.

And thanks to the Border Reivers, without whose massive contribution this book would not have been possible.

Introduction

A 13th-century English enemy described Edward I as 'valiant as a lion, quick to attack and fearing the onslaught of none. But if a lion in pride and ferocity, he is a leopard in fickleness and inconsistency, changing his word and promise, cloaking himself by pleasant speech. When he is cornered he promises whatever you wish, but as soon as he is free he forgets his promise. The treachery or falsehood by which he is advanced he calls prudence; the path by which he attains his ends, however crooked, he calls straight; and whatever he likes he says is lawful.' This then was the man who 'Lit the fuse' – the man who started it all…

But what do you think the Reivers were like?

I asked this question of a friend from the Borders, a historian of some experience, and he told me 'Imagine the hardest, toughest and roughest person you know – think of them being twice as bad and then you have some idea of what the nobility were like!' – hard men indeed – products of a hard and difficult society.

The lives of the Reivers have been romanticised over the years both by writers and through the traditional Border Ballads, which have been handed down through the generations. Reiving was going on constantly against a background of war, religion, politics and everyday life, and indeed it had an effect on all of these to a greater or lesser extent. It must have been a difficult time to live – under constant threat from one family or another or from one nation or another or indeed from those that were intent on upholding the law in their own way.

It is difficult to associate specific families with certain locations because of the constant movement and shifting alliances, a lot of the sites have now fallen into ruin and are not easy to find and some of the locations are totally different from how they were in reiving times.

However, I have tried to present an overview of the way of life on the Borders in those days and also tried to link in many of the sites and events, some well-known and some not so well known, with specially-taken photographs. Britain was really divided into three areas in those days – England, Scotland and the Borders – and the situation was thus for almost 400 years – no wonder it had such a far reaching influence on the area. The Borders is still a wild and rugged area with an unforgettable beauty – it is an independent place and its people have a particular charisma linked with a wonderful sense of humour. The idea of this book is to encourage people to explore the history of the Reivers and to look into their own ancestry and link it with the local history of the area – it does not profess to be an academic work, but I'm sure you will find it as fascinating to read as it was to photograph and write.

While I have been working on this book, I have come across people from many parts of the world who claim some connection with the Borders. There are almost 80 recognised Reiver names from the days of the Border Reivers and all of these can be found in the area today – most people from the north of England and the south of Scotland probably have some connection – but the influence and connection reaches out worldwide, and I would venture that every one of them is extremely proud of their Reiver heritage.

Philip Nixon
2007

The Border Reivers

The Border country has always been a wild area, both in landscape and history. It has seen many years of war and turmoil but is an enchanting area of great beauty and has the capacity to imprint its unique charisma on every visitor. It is undoubtedly a fascinating and wonderfully-romantic area, and yet the bold stories of its bloody history can still chill the soul.

About 400 years ago it was a desperate and dangerous place – this unsettled region precariously separated the continually warring kingdoms of England and Scotland – it was a bitterly lawless land where no man dare venture unarmed, a land where every home was a fortress by necessity because almost every family was at deadly feud, and it was a time when killing, burning, looting, theft, blackmail and robbery had become an accepted way of life for the Armstrongs, the Elliots, the Nixons, the Milburns, the Dodds, the Robsons and the Grahams – the 'Great Riding Families' remembered in history as the Border Reivers!

Home Castle.

Rise of the Reiver

The Border Reiver was a unique figure in English history, and although some of them did live in outlaw bands most of them were scattered throughout the social classes. He could be described variously as a labourer, a gentleman farmer, or even a Peer of the Realm. Irrespective of social standing, he was also a hard-fighting man, a skilled guerrilla soldier and an expert in weapon handling and riding, to whom the arts of theft, raid, tracking and ambush were second nature. He was a highly-organised professional gangster who invented, and perfected, the protection racket, and it is from his lawless activities that we have the words blackmail and bereaved in the English language.

The border between England and Scotland takes roughly the same line that it has done since the 11th or 12th centuries, running diagonally from Berwick-Upon-Tweed to Carlisle, approximately along the line of the Cheviot Hills, although it has been hotly disputed at various times.

In 1018, after the Battle of Careham, the victorious Scots laid claim to all the land on the east side of the country to the north of Berwick. Late in 1157 it was William Rufus who incorporated what had been part of Strathclyde into Cumberland and built Carlisle Castle for its defence. It was an uneasy time and both governments, with an eye to defence, encouraged settlers into the border area with the offer of either land or low rents as an incentive.

The area became over populated because of this generous offer, and this problem was further compounded by a system of partible inheritance known as 'gavelkind'. This had a profound effect on Border economy. The land owned by a father was shared among his sons and divided and subdivided with each subsequent generation, and the holdings eventually became too small to provide a living for their owners – the difficult situation was further exacerbated by poor soil quality and outdated farming methods, not to mention the waves of war that were being waged constantly. Although some of the gentry owned large extents of land and thousands of sheep, many of the peasants struggled to survive and were forced to the edge of starvation, and consequently raiding became a part-time occupation necessary to supplement the family income. Whatever effect it had on the economic circumstances, gavelkind served to strengthen kinship because younger sons were not ousted from the family land. It has even been suggested that this system was encouraged by the gentry in order to maintain a ready supply of troops for Border service. However, it still became a serious problem, and many of the sons of these

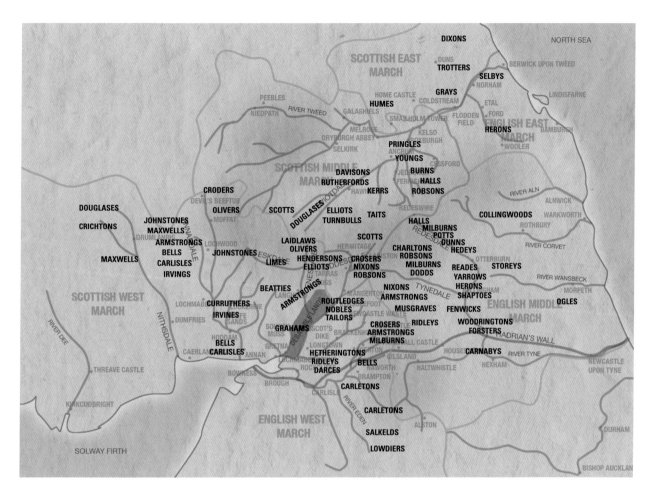

families were forced to seek employment further afield – it is well known that Newcastle firms would not offer apprenticeships to young men from Tynedale because of their reputation as Reivers – in fact this attitude continued into the 20th century.

In spite of national differences, the people who lived on either side of the border had much in common. Living in an inhospitable climate in a wild land bred tough, fearsome and belligerent men, who by their nature were quick to take offence. An attack, or even the slightest insult, on himself or his kinsmen would bring fast, furious and severe retribution because of the single-minded, almost fanatical loyalty to his family and grayne (surname). Law and order managed by the government was far away in the south of the country, and because of the poor levels of justice available to the Borderer he found it necessary to settle his own disputes.

Family feuds, enshrined in a warped code of honour, often smouldered on for years and provoked further periodic eruptions of bitter enmity. The continuous raiding, together with shady, shifting family alliances on both sides of the border, made sure that there was always some incident, no matter how trivial, that would give offence – there was absolutely no excuse not to get into a fight with someone. The ability to survive in what was really a war-zone became the very essence of the Borderers' precarious way of life. Vendetta and bloody feud made these men skilled and ruthless marauders, and they lived in an area where the constant threat of robbery, violence, ambush, skirmish, pursuit and even violent death carried an horrendous inevitability. The outcome was that there was no way to overcome this disturbing situation without the risk of raiding and reiving, and through dreadful necessity this became the only way for men to support their wives and bairns.

Religion had no effect on the character of the Borderers, and even priests carried sword and dagger, a sensible extra precaution for their own safety. Many churches on the Borders were heavily fortified and could be quickly pressed into service to offer protection to congregation or villagers during raids or skirmishes. Bishop Leslie of Ross, the Scottish historian, was quick to acknowledge that religious belief was on the Reivers' own terms and observed that their devotions became ever more intense before setting out on a raid. At christenings the would-be sword hand of the child was left unblessed so that it could strike all-the-better unholy blows on the enemy!

Even if the Reivers had wanted to follow religion to the letter, it would have been difficult. The Reformation caused a considerable drop in the number of clergy, and it became more and more difficult to find men who would face the dangers in the Borders even to serve God. This unfortunate situation gave rise to two customs particular to the area. The first was a 'Book-a-Bosom Parson', who got his name because he travelled around the Borders with the Book of Mass in the inside pocket of his clothing, holding services, marriages and christenings on his periodic visits to each bastle, tower, farm or settlement. Burials did not seem to cause too many problems because, for instance, many families, such as the Armstrongs of Hollows, buried their dead in their towers, but a large number of Reivers were destined to end up on the gallows anyway.

The second custom was a direct result of the first: if a couple wished to get married the chances were that the event did not always coincide with the priest's visit and a tradition called 'handfasting' developed. A couple would live together until the itinerant priest made his visit and could bless their union. It was a trial period for one year, after which it became permanent; however, if either party wished to end the arrangement before a year had passed they would still be responsible for any children that were born, so their children were still regarded as legitimate. Nobody in the Borders was particularly concerned about children born out of wedlock, and there are many instances of men making mention of their natural children in their wills, but if they were not amply provided for, and having no land to farm, these youngsters would swell the ranks of the broken men whose only occupation and income was reiving.

The Reivers regarded the church and its servants with the same contempt as everyone else – no one was safe. Acomb, which belonged to the estates of the Archbishop of York, was burned during one serious raid, and he retaliated with a swift and bitter excommunication. Richard Fox, the Prince Bishop of Durham, was the next one to be upset with a series of repeated raids into his bishopric by the men of Tynedale and Redesdale. He was also pushed to pronounce excommunication, although he did offer to re-admit the Reivers to the church if they repented! The clergy were also lambasted by Bishop Fox – he accused them of not being able to read or understand the bible, said they were scruffy and dirty in appearance, and he even suggested they were not properly ordained and were unfit to administer sacraments to the thieves and robbers in Northumberland. In fact, things had become so bad that Cardinal Wolsey was moved to put 'that evil country' under interdict. heidman Hector Charlton found this amusing and persuaded an itinerant Scottish priest to say Mass, while he himself served the communion wine.

Things were no better in Scotland, and it got steadily worse, culminating in drastic action. An excommunication was bad enough, but Gavin Dunbar, the Archbishop of Glasgow, decided to go a step further – he laid an extreme and comprehensive curse or commination on the Scottish Reivers. He was wholehearted in his wish to punish them because a curse, once given, could not be undone. It was read from every pulpit in the land and went on for 1,500 words, putting the good Archbishop among the greatest cursers of all time.

The Scottish Reivers, of course, just laughed at his efforts, just as their opposite numbers on the other side of the border had laughed at excommunication and interdict.

To the Riding families life was simply a matter of survival of the fittest – raid and be raided – they rode with an arrogant disregard for the law and both governments realised that these constant hostilities had created a dangerous and unstable society. Something had to be done, and in an attempt to create some sort of order from the chaos they came to an agreement in 1249 known as 'The Leges Marchiarum' or 'The Laws of the Marches'. Under its terms, both sides of the border were divided into three areas, the East, West and Middle Marches, and by 1297 a March warden had been appointed to each to govern and police the unruly inhabitants. Furthermore, because the standard laws of the land were proving to be inadequate, Border Laws were introduced covering such specifics as aiding raids into ones native country and illegal marriage to someone in the opposite realm; these laws also provided for the lawful recovery of stolen goods.

King Alexander II of Scotland was killed in a riding accident when he fell over a cliff in 1286. Edward I, with ever an eye for expansion and in particular an ambition to control Scotland, took advantage of the situation, and in the absence of an adult heir to the Scottish throne he used his influence to appoint John Baliol in the role of puppet ruler, but unfortunately he upset Robert the Bruce in the process. Edward's overbearing attitude toward the Scots became intolerable and led to a revolt – the Treaty of Revolt between Scotland and France soon followed. Edward was furious and exacted a terrible revenge by launching a simultaneous sea and land attack on Berwick. The sea attack was repulsed, but through subterfuge Edward's army gained entry and overran the town. On Good Friday 1296, some historians say, he ordered over 17,000 men, women and children to be put to the sword – they say the streets ran red with blood for almost a week afterwards, and, as an encore, he burned the town to ashes, earning himself the dubious title of 'The Hammer of the Scots'.

By July 1296 Edward confirmed his conquest by plundering Scotland's Royal Regalia. He took the Black Rood of Margaret, Scotland's Holiest relic, and the Stone of Scone – also called the Stone of Destiny – and took them to Westminster Abbey.

By further devastation Edward hoped to pacify the Scots, but what actually happened was William Wallace, whose timely victory over the English at Stirling Bridge rallied the nation. Together with his patriotic army, they mounted a retaliation of equal ferocity and devastation, driving deep into Northern England with fire and sword.

Eventually Edward defeated Wallace at the Battle of Falkirk in 1298. Wallace fled to France, but when he returned in 1305 he was betrayed and executed. Robert the Bruce claimed the throne in 1306 and was helped by two events in his fight for freedom: Edward I died in 1307 and his feckless and effeminate son Edward II immediately succeeded him to the throne. Edward II and Robert the Bruce came head to head at the Battle of Bannockburn in 1314, which resulted in a resounding and defining victory for the Scots, a victory that was to re-establish and confirm Scotland as an independent kingdom. Robert the Bruce and his victorious army then systematically ravaged the English Marches. Sporadic attacks and counter attacks, invasion and counter invasion ensued until, in 1513, open hostilities between the two countries erupted again with an English invasion of France and a Scottish invasion of England.

The incursions and counter incursions continued until hostilities came to a head at what was, perhaps, the greatest Border battle: Flodden Field in 1513, when the Earl of Surrey defeated the Scots. King James IV and much of the Scottish nobility were killed. It was a catastrophe for Scotland and periods of uneasy truce followed right through the 1520s.

In spite of, or indeed because of, these circumstances, the Borderers may well have questioned their national identity – it was understandable because their allegiance lay with each other and not their respective governments. Politics and social instability bred a community which distrusted outsiders and other nationalities, part of an unsophisticated society whose traditions were moulded by international warfare, local conflicts and poverty. Coupled with the fact that the lower classes were almost uneducated and that illiteracy among the gentry was quite common, it gives a feeling for the understanding of the pressures and circumstances that moulded the character of the Border Reivers.

Robert the Bruce.

Robert the Bruce

On 10 February 1306 Robert Bruce killed John Comyn of Badenoch – 'The Red Comyn' – aided by Sir Roger Kirkpatrick in the Kirk of Grey Friars Monastery and so started the final stage of the Scottish War of Independence. With this act of sacrilege and murder, Bruce catapulted himself to the front of the Scottish political scene at a time when Edward I had, or so he thought, at last completed the English conquest of Scotland.

Six weeks later Bruce was crowned at Scone – a ceremony veiled as a symbol of national defiance because every Scot knew that Edward had removed the sacred Stone of Scone.

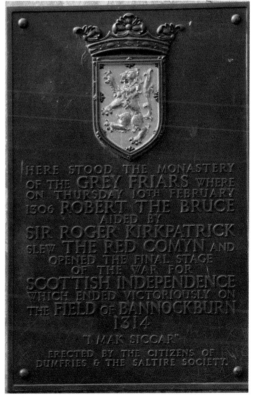

Robert the Bruce plaque, Dumfries.

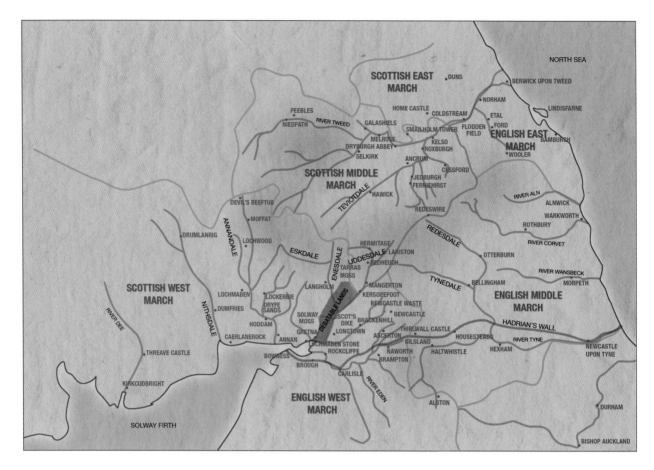

Border Marches

The Scottish East March occupied what was, in effect, the eastern side of Berwickshire and took in the fertile stretch of land known as The Merse. It covered that section of the borderline from Berwick to the Hanging Stone on the Cheviot. It was largely dominated by the Home family, who mainly operated from their fortress at Home Castle, together with other strongholds such as Fast Castle, which enjoyed a seemingly impregnable position on the coast.

The English East March lay directly opposite its Scottish equivalent and included all the north-eastern parts of Northumberland, as well as those sections of the Palatinate of Durham known as Norhamshire and Islandshire, which were, of course, of the utmost importance to the Prince Bishop of Durham. The mighty castles of Norham and Wark defended the vitally important crossings of the Tweed here. Berwick was where the warden had his headquarters and was described at that time as 'the strongest hold in Britain'. The Herons, Greys and Selbys were the most important families here, ruled by the influence of the Earls of Northumberland.

The broad flat area of the coastal

plain offered the opportunity of easy passage for invading armies, and consequently this area suffered at the hands of both nations.

Drumlanrig's Tower, Hawick

Drumlanrig's Tower is Hawick's oldest surviving building and stands on the eastern bank of the Slitrig Water just above the point where it flows into the River Teviot. The tower now serves as a comprehensive tourist information centre and houses an excellent museum. It was originally built

Border exhibition, Drumlanrig's Tower.

around the middle of the 16th century by the Douglases of Drumlanrig, who used it as a centre of administration for the area as well as a family residence. In the latter part of the 16th century it passed into the

Drumlanrig's Tower, Hawick.

The Horse, Hawick.

ownership of the Scotts of Buccleuch and Branxholme.

On many occasions during the 15th and 16th centuries, Hawick suffered cross border raids by the English. However, a local story tells of how, just after the Battle of Flodden in 1514, the men of Hawick took revenge by completely routing a party of English and capturing their standard – this proud event in local history is commemorated by a memorial, *The Horse*, which has pride of place in the main street. This remarkable event is celebrated annually in June by one of the oldest Border Common Ridings.

The Scottish Middle March took in the rest of Berwickshire and the whole of Roxburghshire, extending as far north as Peebles which, probably due to its great distance from the border,

managed to stay remarkably free from English raids. Kelso, Hawick and Jedburgh were more attractive targets and got more than their fair share. The justice courts were usually held in Jedburgh, and 'Jeddart Justice' was to become well-known and greatly feared throughout the Borders. Usually the warden's duties fell to the Kerrs, who had strongholds at nearby Ferniehirst and Cessford. Originally, this march included Teviotdale and Liddesdale – the home of the Elliots, the Armstrongs and their associates, described as 'the great surnames and most offensive to England'. These families launched some of the biggest and most savage raids into English East and Middle Marches and consequently became known as some of the most feared and notorious raiders in the Borders.

Because these valleys were so remote, making it very difficult for wardens to mount reprisal raids, it was necessary to appoint an extra warden known as 'The Keeper of Liddesdale', who administered justice from the sinister and remote Hermitage Castle. These were tough men by necessity and included the lairy and unsettling James Hepburn, the 4th Earl of Bothwell, and the charismatic but dangerous Sir Walter Scott of Buccleuch.

Eildon Hills

The Eildon Hills are a distinctive landmark visible from much of the Border country.

Eildon Hills from Ancrum Moor.

The English Middle March covered the western side of Northumberland and incorporated the districts of Tynedale and Redesdale. In the market town of Hexham, Tynedale had the distinction of having the first purpose-built gaol in England – however, good gaols were few and far between and those that were available were generally in such an insecure and ruinous state that unless they were strongly guarded they were almost useless. Tynedale was so bad that it was well known as a wild and unruly place where the power of the law was notably non-existent. The March was administered from Alnwick with strong garrisons at Harbottle and Chipchase, and although the Cheviot Hills were a difficult obstacle for regular troops and artillery the Reivers found access to be no problem – it probably proved to be an easier alternative than trying to cross the more heavily defended fords over the Tweed.

The Ogles, Fenwicks, Collingwoods and Widdringtons helped to defend against the Scots and, on occasion, against the Charltons, the Robsons, Dodds and Milburns of Tynedale and Redesdale.

Old Border Gaol, Hexham

The Old Gaol at Hexham is thought to be the earliest documented purpose-built prison in England. It was built on the orders of the Archbishop of York between 1330 and 1333 and was used to house prisoners from all over Hexhamshire, and, in the 1500s, prisoners captured in the English Middle March awaiting their trials, which would have been held in the nearby Moothall Court Room. The museum provides an excellent insight into the lives of the Border Reivers, and through its important collections a lot of

Eildon Hills from Ancrum Moor.

Hexham Border Gaol.

information is available relating to the unique culture of the Borders, especially Tynedale.

One item of macabre interest, although it is not strictly from reiving times, is the famous Fenwick skull. It is thought to be that of Sir John Fenwick, who was killed at the Battle of Marston Moor in 1644, and came to the museum many years ago. The story goes that it soon decided on a favourite room, and no matter where it was moved to the skull would return there – no one knew how it managed to move between rooms and even floors.

The Fenwick skull.

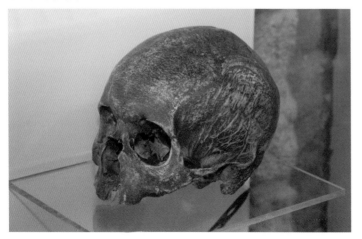

The Scottish West March was made up of the Stewartries of Kirkcudbright and Annandale, together with the Sheriffdom of Dumfries. The area was dominated by the powerful Maxwell family who had their headquarters at the unusual Caerlaverock Castle near the mouth of the River Nith and also at Lochmaben Castle, which was also elaborately protected by water. The Johnstones of Lochwood and Dryfe also served as wardens when the balance of power altered, as it frequently did; their feud with the Maxwells was possibly the bloodiest and longest in Border history. This was also an unruly area that warranted its own 'Keeper of Annandale', who was based at Langholm Castle.

The English West March covered

Cumberland and Westmorland. In the early days the wardens were the Lords Dacre, who managed to exercise a certain measure of control over the area, but by the end of the 16th century their power had faded and the Lords Scrope began to exert their influence. The headquarters of the March were the mighty castles of Carlisle and Naworth, with garrisons at Bewcastle, Rockcliffe and Askerton. The March bordered the Solway Firth in the north, and although there were a number of fords these could be extremely dangerous, and so the easiest way to mount forays was through Kershope Foot, which was, as Sir Robert Bowes described it, 'a common passage for thieves with stolen goods from one realm to the other'. The families of Salkeld, Musgrove, Lowther and Carleton filled most of the official positions in the English West March, although when some of the families are considered it would be difficult to decide just whose side they were really on.

Larriston Fell

Larriston Fell once echoed to the sound of hoof beats by moonlight, but now the only sounds are the running water, the call of the curlew and the grouse on the sighing wind.

The Debateable Land was between the borders of the two Western Marches marked by the line of the River Sark and Liddel Water. Although it was a

Larriston Fell.

small area, only measuring 12 miles by about five miles, 60 square miles in all, it caused as much trouble as any other area in the Borders.

The area was first mentioned in 1450 – it belonged to neither side, but both English and Scots would pasture their livestock here; however, if anyone tried to build here terrific violence erupted. Neither country would take any responsibility for any incidents that took place here, and the area soon became an unofficial sanctuary for all sorts of dangerous law breakers.

Naturally the Armstrongs, Littles and Bells found refuge here. The notorious Grahams relished the situation and would use it to their great advantage by mounting raids on both the English and the Scots with impunity – seeking refuge in the Debateable Land when redress was sought by the wardens. The situation became intolerable, and in 1551 a commission was set up by both countries to solve the problem. After much difficult discussion, the French ambassador was asked to mediate and an agreement was reached. An earthen rampart known as 'The Scots Dyke' was erected on a line running from the River Esk just below its junction with Liddel Water to the River Sark, which it would follow to the Solway Firth. Each end was marked by a square stone bearing the arms of Scotland on one side and those of England on the other.

The border was now defined – but in spite of the wardens' best efforts the situation stayed exactly the same.

March Wardens

The government of the Border Marches was in the hands of the wardens. They were first mentioned around 1300 and in the early days there was only one warden on either side of the border, but deputies were soon appointed to assist with their duties. As time went on it became more practical to appoint a warden to each of the Marches, and the system grew to include deputy wardens, keepers, land sergeants and bailiffs as responsibilities became wider. Initially the wardens' main duty was defence, but as time went on they gradually acquired a whole range of commitments, such as the capture of criminals and dispensation of justice. In theory, the law of the land was administered by the Justice Courts and the warden was only responsible for trying those offences that had been committed against the specific Border laws. In practice, however, he was largely left to his own devices and administered a kind of martial law. He had absolute power in his own area to administer life and death over his people – if anyone was caught red handed he could dispense summary execution by gallows or pit.

This was rough justice, but there was little time available within the conditions he worked to collect evidence, but the Reivers were quite familiar with this system and knew what to expect if they were caught breaking the law.

His other duties included attempting to prevent raids, including those from his own area, and mounting reprisals when this was unsuccessful, mounting and maintaining watches, keeping defences in good order, making sure that Borderers took part in the hue and cry when requested and holding Truce Days with his opposite number across the border.

On the English side the men appointed mainly as wardens were those who could be kept under tight control by the monarch – in fact, three of the English wardens were closely related to Queen Elizabeth I. This control was seen as a necessary safety precaution because the monarchy had suffered from Northern English Rebellions in the past and the powerful local noble families, such as the Percies, were seen as a potentially dangerous threat.

Warwick the Kingmaker, John of Gaunt and Richard of Gloucester (who became Richard III) all served their time as wardens – Sir John Forster and Lord William Dacre stand out as the only truly local wardens on the English side. The Duke of Norfolk summed up the situation when he said to Henry VIII 'To keep the wild people of all three marches in order will require men of good estimation and nobility.'

The difference between the appointment of English and Scottish wardens was quite significant. The Scots were usually local men because the Scottish government saw this as an advantage – these men knew both the area and the people – however, it could be argued that this was also a disadvantage – they could be heavily involved in blood feuds and had already forged alliances with particular families. The government turned a blind eye to this because they needed loyalty, and they felt that if men like the Maxwells, the Homes and the Douglases could do the job and keep some sort of order and stay loyal then past transgressions such as treason and rebellion could be forgiven.

The Scottish Borderers had an inherent dislike for outside wardens, as in the case of the Frenchman Anthony Darcy, 'the Sieur de la Bastie', who in 1516 boldly accepted the position of warden of the Eastern Scottish March. He performed his conscientious duty with bravery and honesty, which probably served to sow the seeds of dislike and distrust.

The Homes harboured enormous distrust and jealousy against outsiders and Darcy was ruthlessly ambushed, his head hacked off and hung on the Mercat Cross in Duns as a grim warning.

There was a constant state of tension between the two countries, and it necessarily followed that the wardens of either country did not fully trust each other; the constant spying on each other in case invasion was being planned, not to mention agents from other countries being present in the Borders, made the warden's job even more difficult, coupled with the fact that there was not always a strong force of regular troops available to assist, and wardens of both sides had to rely on keeping in favour with the powerful local landowners and Hiedmen.

The office carried with it a large degree of personal danger; for example, four wardens were killed in office between 1511 and 1600 – coupled with this was the ever-present danger that a deadly feud between families could stir up at any time, taking into account the nature and disposition of the character of the average Borderer.

Given the nature of the job, a March warden was probably one of the best governors in history, but they still complained bitterly about the remuneration for the post, although they did receive expenses and lived in an official residence free of rent.

The Scottish wardens would earn about £100 per year, but this would vary – in the tough West March the pay could be as high as £500 and the Keeper of Liddesdale could earn £1,200, although this salary was extremely hard-earned!

The English salaries ranged between £300 and £1,100 – this was also considered poor – Elizabeth I enjoyed a reputation of being 'very canny' with her money in relation to the salaries of most of her officials.

However, the position of warden carried power and prestige and the finances could be supplemented by other means. One of the best ways to do this was to mount a Warden's Roade – this was a large-scale raid across the border supposedly to gain redress against persistent raiders from the opposite realm.

The warden was legally entitled to half the value of all the plunder and half the value of the ransom for prisoners brought back – the other half, of course, went to the Crown.

He was also entitled to a percentage of 'the unlaws' or fines imposed in the Wardens' Courts, which in some circumstances could be considerable.

In Scotland the warden could use his power and vast influence to enrich himself and his family and to secure his property against his enemies – his power in the March was absolute and any profit came to him.

Redheuch ~ Liddesdale

Upper Liddesdale was home to the Nobles, who produced the famous Hobbie Noble, the Elliots, the Bells and the Nixons, including

Redheuch.

that arch-villain Cuddie Nixon, probably better known as 'Blanketlugs'.

The Hot Trod

In the event of a raid the Borderer who had been 'spoylt', as it was termed, had several choices: he could lodge a complaint with his March warden and hope that justice would be done under the Border laws, or he could make a plan with his family and associates to mount a return raid on those who had robbed him.

The other alternative was to mount a pursuit to recover his stolen goods by force and to deal out any immediate and violent punishment to the thieves. This was a legal and well-respected process known as either 'The Hote Troade', Hot Trod, or 'The Cold Troade', Cold Trod. The Hot Trod was carried out immediately and the Cold Trod would be mounted at a later time, but had to be within six days of the raid.

The rules were carefully laid out under Border laws to distinguish between a Trod and a Reprisal Raid; the Borderer was entitled to enlist the support of his neighbours – they were obliged to assist and ride with him – and few men refused because failure to 'follow the fray' was punishable by seven days in prison and a fine of 3s 4d. Fortunately this had been reduced from the death penalty it carried in the 1550s.

Those men who assisted on the Trod were rewarded with a percentage of the value of goods recovered – 1s in the pound for those recovered in England and 2s in the pound for those recovered in Scotland.

A Trod would be an impressive sight: the tracking dogs or 'slewe hounds' would be turned loose and the riders would be accompanied by the sounding of a horn, and one of the riders would hold aloft a piece of burning turf on the tip of his lance, the flames fanned by the speed of the riders. This was the 'Lawfull Trodd with Horse and Hound, with Hue and Cry, and all other accustomed manner of fresh pursuit' described in the 1563 agreement between England and Scotland.

Most importantly, perhaps, the Trod was legally allowed to cross the border fully armed, their only obligation was to inform the first person or the first village they encountered of their purpose and intent, called 'The Witnessing of a Trod'. This person would be obliged to join the pursuit because the 'Troblance of a Troade' was a serious offence and the offender would be held legally liable for the value of the stolen goods.

It would usually seem that the men who followed the Trod had the initial advantage because the raiders would have to travel slowly because of the livestock they had stolen and would be weighed down with stolen plunder. However, their extensive knowledge of the countryside they were crossing would mean that they could lose themselves and their stolen livestock with effortless ease.

Sometimes the raiders would lie in wait and ambush their pursuers and a bloody fight would determine the outcome. But, if the Trod was successful, the raiders would be captured and either taken back and held for ransom or delivered into the custody of the March warden. In some instances, the raiders were killed in cold blood or hanged on the spot – this was known as 'beene taken with the read hande', or caught red-handed, another expression in the English Language that comes from the Reivers. On the spot hangings and executions probably concluded many a successful Trod, but it was highly unlikely that the law would punish a Trod-follower if things got out of hand in the heat of the moment.

Days of Truce

The arrangements made for dealing with offences against Border law may seem primitive, but they were by no means ineffective – with all things considered they were probably as good as could have been devised in the difficult circumstances.

Since offences against the law were numerous and frequent, it was decided that 'A Day Of Truce', sometimes also known as a Triste or Steven, extending from sunrise of the agreed day to the sunrise of the next, should be held once a month, or more often if possible, when the wardens of the opposite Marches should meet for discussion and adjustment of their respective claims and, of course, to dispense punishment to the various law-breakers.

The date and place of these meetings was made known to the people of the Marches by an announcement by proclamation in all the market towns. Those who had complaints against men in the opposite March lodged their 'bills of complaynt' with their warden, and the wardens would then forward the bills to each other. It was the duty of the wardens to summon the accused to the Day of Truce and to make sure that any previously convicted men should appear to answer for their crimes.

Notice was sent to all the lords, knights and heidmen, commanding them to assemble a well-armed and mounted retinue of their servants and tenants to attend the meeting. On the day this great cavalcade would make its way to the rendezvous, which was usually some convenient place near the border and most often on the Scottish side.

Several places became traditional venues: Kershopefoot, the Lochma-benstone and the English Rockcliffe on the West March; Cocklaw, Gamelspath and Redeswire on the Middle March and Norham Ford on the Tweed, Carham, Coldstream and Wark on the East March.

As the custom dictated, when the wardens came within hailing distance of each other a halt was called. The English warden then sent three or four of his most respected riders forward to ask that an assurance of peace would be given until the following sunrise. This was vital because it meant that everyone would reach home in safety before the truce ended. On some occasions extra time may have been requested depending on the number of cases to be heard. After the Scottish warden had given his assurance he would then send some of his own specially selected riders to ask the same favour of the English warden. Only then would they salute each other by raising their right hands – the two parties then met and the business that had brought them together was started. If, for any reason, a March warden was unable to attend the meeting, the responsibility would then fall to the deputy warden, although these were usually highly-respected men of great influence and good social position who were well qualified to deal with any problems that may arise.

A Truce Day was also a social event and there would be stalls set out selling all kinds of goods. Adding to the fair-like atmosphere, pedlars, piemen, broggers, badgers, cadgers and tinklers would all take the opportunity to make money at the gathering. Old scores and feuds would be laid aside, although it would, perhaps, be prudent to keep a wary eye on old enemies. Talk would be about the forthcoming bills and their outcome. Games of cards and dice would be played and perhaps even a football match, and there might also have been the opportunity to do a little horse dealing. Those attending would probably be wearing their finest clothes,

but all would be armed as in Border tradition, but no one would expect to use their weapons on such an important social occasion.

Regulations for the conduct of business were carefully drawn out and strictly observed. A jury would be carefully chosen, six Englishmen by the Scottish warden and six Scots chosen by the English warden. Only honourable men were supposed to serve; 'traytors, murderers, fugitives, and betrayers', along with other dishonest persons, were rejected – this in itself must have reduced the selection somewhat!

Oaths would be sworn and the business of the day begun. Bills were presented in detail and the prisoners or the accused were called upon to answer the charges. There were several methods by which the bills were tried: one well-used method was by jury – the English charges were considered by the Scots and, of course, vice versa. Another method was by 'Wardens Oath' – he would swear on his honour as to the validity of the evidence, proving either the guilt or innocence of the plaintiff. The other method was for an independent witness or 'A vower', who had to be accepted by both parties, to swear on the truth of the evidence.

Somewhat similar to this, but much more ancient, and, by then, only heard of in connection with church matters, was the method of compurgation, where three uninvolved witnesses would make a communal oath as to the innocence or guilt of the accused party.

Dishonesty by a Borderer when testifying, or indeed any instance where he failed to keep his word of honour, would result in suffering public reproof in the form of 'bauchling'. At a Truce Day, or any public gathering, a glove would be held aloft on the point of a lance – this represented the false hand of the accused – and in some extreme cases the spear and glove would be fixed to the roof of his house to draw attention to his treachery.

If a bogus bill was filed there was statutory provision for the persons guilty of this offence to be handed over to the opposite warden to be punished, imprisoned and fined at the discretion of the warden he had tried to deceive.

When a bill was filed the amount of compensation had to be carefully calculated and the guilty party was often required to pay a three-fold penalty of 'principall, doubles, and sawfie'. Principall was the basic value of goods stolen or injury compensation due. Doubles was the original value added again – in reality a fine imposed by the warden – and Sawfie was the original amount added yet again to cover administration costs and the collection expenses.

If the accused was unable to pay the fine then his heidman or member of his family would be asked to stand as a pledge until the fine was paid or the goods were returned – failure to meet this obligation within a year and a day would result in the pledge being put to death. Understandably, perhaps, not a lot of people volunteered for this position and often the warden had to 'arrest' the wrongdoer and warn him of the severe consequences he would suffer if he did not turn up at the next Truce Day.

If the offender could not be found and no one would come forward, then he would be outlawed by the ceremony of 'blowing out' or 'Putting to the horn' – not for the crime he had committed but because nobody would stand as a pledge for him – he was then automatically classed as a 'broken man'. His breaking was signalled by a proclamation accompanied by the sound of a horn at all the market crosses in the March.

The most dramatic outcome of a Border meeting was the pronounce-ment of the death penalty. The guilty persons would be taken away to suffer death by hanging on the gallows or drowning in the pit – their deaths would be proclaimed as 'an example to parents to bring up their children in the fear of God and the obedience of the Laws of the Realm'.

The meeting was drawn to a close when a proclamation was read announcing the findings of the court and then everyone would return to their homes in their respective marches.

Finally, the duty of each warden was to collect the sums of money owing from the offenders in his own area and pay out the required amounts owed to the individual claimants.

Although the Days of Truce and Border meetings were a good idea in principle, the reality was a little less satisfactory. It was not unknown for a warden to 'shoot' a meeting – that is not turn up when it was arranged – Sir John Forster, the wily old English warden, was renowned for his cunning and regular application of this ploy to suit his own ends. The Earl of Angus was so skilled in these tactics that he had official complaints lodged about his behaviour.

With Ker of Cessford this 'clarting about' reached such an intense level that the English government lodged a complaint against him, and King James had to intervene. Further royal intervention was necessary in the late 1500s when Lord Henry Scrope in the East March and Sir John Forster in the West March had both been unable to arrange successful meetings with their respective counterparts.

Furthermore, it is thought that over a quarter of Days of Truce during the reign of Queen Elizabeth I failed to take place. Understandable, perhaps, when it is taken into consideration that between 1511 and 1600 four wardens were murdered while in office. And, of course, by the last decade of the 16th century a succession of bad harvests had resulted in famine and death, contributing to the escalating lawlessness, and reiving in the Borders began to spiral out of control.

The Reivers and their way of life

The necessary allegiance to family and the constant state of war and turmoil along the border shaped the everyday

lives of the people. Living depended largely on livestock rather than crops, and their agricultural system followed a regular pattern. Raiding took place all the year round, but it was more popular from autumn to spring when the nights were longer. It also took place in the summer, but it was far less systematic then because time was devoted to growing crops such as barley, oats and rye. However, most time and effort was given to raising cattle and sheep. In April the Borderer would move up to the higher ground, living in his sheiling for four or five months while his beasts were pastured. These summer communities were a little safer than their winter homes but were still, on occasion, subject to raids. This nomadic life, as William Camden the noted historian and map maker called it, suited the Borderers well – they had learned from years of living through raiding and wars not to build permanent dwellings but to live constantly on the move.

Reivers probably lived largely on broth with a little beef or mutton. Bishop Leslie commented extensively on their diet, referring to them eating mostly 'flesh, milk and boiled barley' and that bread was only eaten rarely, but that 'hearth cakes of oats' were eaten instead. He said that the Borderers took very little beer or wine, which is probably why drunken behaviour gets few mentions in the Border records.

Both men and women on the Borders dressed to a standard they could afford, although the emphasis must necessarily have been on the practical and the hard wearing. However, some style and finery must have been in evidence judging by the descriptions given of items of stolen clothing in the complaints lodged with the March wardens on Truce Days.

The women were usually well treated and highly respected and were said to be generally regarded as being of a fair and comely disposition. An unwritten law in the Reivers' code forbade the attack and violation of women, and rape was an uncommon crime.

There are many references to the strong-minded women who made their presence felt, and one particular tale tells of how the women of the Charlton family would traditionally serve a 'dish of spurs' to the head of the family indicating that the larder was empty and it was time to be riding.

By and large the children were well looked after and were raised in the strong tradition of their family surnames, but unfortunately childhood did not last very long and there is a record of an 11-year-old Johnson taking part in a raid.

By way of indoor recreation, the Reivers enjoyed poetry and music which was, in fact, closely associated in the singing of the traditional Border Ballads to the accompaniment of the harp or the small pipes. These ballads were epics which were handed down by word of mouth – they were nearly always tragic, had occasional flashes of humour but, as a rule, had very few happy endings. Perhaps this sadness and melancholy was understandable considering the way of life they pursued.

But music and poetry were not the only pastimes, and during the hours of darkness, when there was no particular urge to go on a raid, the time would be wiled away playing cards, dice or at the tables (backgammon). Gambling was a great passion that was in the blood, again probably fuelled by the lifestyle, and many a horse or beast, hard won on a moonlight raid, must have changed hands during the course of these games.

Hawking, hunting and fishing also provided suitable sport for the gentry when they were not raiding or fighting, while lesser men would fish and course hares, although there were restrictions to this particular pastime introduced in 1605, precluding the very poor.

Football was another sport greatly enjoyed by everyone, but at one time the Scottish authorities tried to ban it because they said it interfered with archery practice. The Armstrongs of Liddesdale were always keen to arrange matches against other families in games that would often go on from dawn to dusk, with no restrictions on numbers, sides or rules, and were only interrupted when fights broke out or because of broken limbs. The Armstrongs of Whithaugh arranged what is thought to be the first six-a-side match in history, played at Bewcastle against six local English lads. However, one of the Ridleys, keen to capture the notorious Armstrongs on English soil,

Denton Bastle from the churchyard.

got his associates together to spring an ambush.

Upper Denton, near Gilsland

Upper Denton near Gilsland is only a few miles from the border and would have been a probable target for Scottish raiders. St Cuthbert's Church on the northern edge of the hamlet is said to be of Saxon origin but with Norman influence – some of the stones used in its construction came from the nearby Birdoswald Roman Fort. On the edge of the churchyard is a fine example of a bastle house, probably used as a refuge by the incumbent in times of danger –

Denton Church.

Denton Bastle.

religious buildings were an attractive proposition for raiders and offered an easy target with good reward. Even the clergy were not safe from the large-scale raiding that went on in this area, on the edge of Bewcastle Waste.

Unfortunately, the Armstrongs were tipped off and Ridley and his men were set upon by over 200 riders – Ridley and two of his friends were killed and over 30 men were taken prisoner and, it says in the record, 'Many were sore hurt – especially John Whytfield whose bowells came out but are sowed up again.' In the excitement and intensity of the aftermath, no one remembered to record the result of the match…

However, horse racing was probably the most popular recreation with the Reivers and events were held throughout the Borders – like football,

these meetings were frowned upon by the authorities because it was always suspected that raids and other acts of skulduggery were planned under the cover of these events.

There is no evidence to suggest that huge sums of money were offered as prizes, but winners were rewarded with a bell, which took the place of a cup – but heavy gambling on the outcome of races was inevitable, of course. Racehorses were greatly prized, and even though horse-trading between countries was largely forbidden the Reivers were prepared to disregard this inconvenience as far as a good animal was concerned. In one well-known incident Humphrey Musgrave, warden of the West March, entered his horse, Bay Sandford, in a race in Liddesdale so that Armstrong of Mangerton might assess its performance; the horse was successful and won three bells, and Armstrong bought the animal – despite the feud that raged between the two men and the fact that the warden had arrested Armstrong in his own home only a short time previously!

The majority of ordinary people in the Borders lived in houses that could be regarded as makeshift because they could be built in a very short time. A number of wooden stakes would be driven into the ground and the gaps would be filled in with stones and turf sods. These walls were finished off with clay and the roof would be either turf or thatch. Wooden shutters were provided to keep out the worst of the weather and the doorway was probably hung with a section of cow hide. These huts could be built in about three or four hours – probably just as well when it is considered how frequently they would be raided and destroyed.

In the larger villages, or indeed the smaller towns, more permanent houses could be built. Some would have half-stone walls, but they were just as likely to be constructed from massive oak timbers, strongly mortared and thickly lined and roofed with turf to render them almost fireproof, which would, hopefully, deter the casual raider.

The Bastle House was really a fortified farm house about 40ft long and about 20ft wide and built to two storeys with walls of rough hewn stone between 4ft and 5ft thick. In times of danger livestock would enter the safety of the ground floor through a door, possibly in the gable end. In the early days the inhabitants' entry to the upper floor would be by ladder through an access hole, but later more convenient exterior stone staircases were added. A fireplace at one end of the wooden-floored upper room would provide warmth, while scant relief from the gloom was provided by small narrow windows. Some historians believe that the name bastle is derived from the French word for fortress, bastille.

The pele tower was, perhaps, the most impressive and functional defensive building in the Borders. Many can still be seen and have been renovated and converted to private and comfortable homes.

These towers were built by the lairds and heidmen to three or four storeys with the emphasis very much on personal safety, constructed in solid stone and the walls were up to 10ft thick. The entrance was a double door on ground level; one would be made of oak reinforced with iron and the other was a thick, heavy iron grating known as a yett. The ground floor would be used for storage and possibly for the protection of livestock.

The living floors above were reached by a narrow spiral staircase called a turnpike, which wound its way upwards in a clockwise fashion – in theory making it easier for the man defending because he would have his unguarded left side to the wall, leaving his sword arm free.

On the roof of the house a walkway would provide the opportunity for a lookout to patrol, and there would also be a beacon which could be lit to summon help during an attack or to give warning of an impending raid. Pele towers were simple and strong and the occupants could hold out against a force of superior numbers for long periods. The tower was often surrounded by an extensive stone wall known as a 'barmkin' – this would be about 8ft high and over 2ft thick – and this compound offered further protection to people and livestock during the all-too-frequent raids.

A pele was so well built that, even if the occupants left its protection to hide in the surrounding hills or mosses in the face of a large scale attack, they could pack it with peat which would be ignited and left to smoulder for days, preventing the attackers from entering to cause massive destruction. After the attackers' interests had subsided and the owners returned, they would only have to repair or replace the burned woodwork – the smouldering peat would have had no effect on the stone of the massive tower.

Reiver Names and Nicknames or To-names

Family unity was one of the things that was typical of the Borders and, indeed, made them different from the rest of England and Scotland. The surnames, or graynes, tended to settle in particular valleys and dales, and although this was beneficial in terms of strength of numbers and safety it gave rise to a problem of personal identification because successive generations used the same Christian names. Because of this, the Borderers developed their own particular solution to the problem by giving each other nicknames, or 'to-names', to further assist identification of the individual. There were numerous Jock Armstrongs, Hob Elliots, Dand Fosters, Richie Grahams and Walter Scotts. One method of distinguishing individuals was by alluding to people by their father's name in addition to their own, in the old Cumbrian tradition. Thus, we get Jock's Sandy, Richie's Will, Dand's Sim and Will's Christie.

This was sometimes extended to a third generation to further distinguish individuals and produced names such as Jock's Christie's Jock, Sandy's Geordie's Archie, Gibb's Dand's Johnnie and Dick's Davies Davy.

The mother's name was also used in some circumstances – possibly when a birth had been posthumous or perhaps where a handfasting had not been followed by a marriage – and so names like Jenet's Watte, Nanse's Archie and Bessie's Christie were used. And, just as Jock the Laird's son could be known as 'The Laird's Jock', a Laird's widow's son may be known as 'The Lady's Hob'.

Another method used was adding the name of a man's place of residence to his Christian name, and so names like Jock 'o the Side, Garvie of the Hill, Cuddie of Brankhouse, Sim of the Cathills and Dand of Baghead were used.

However, the most interesting, and perhaps the ones that gave the Borderers the most pleasure, were the colourfully descriptive and often highly offensive names that referred to personal appearance, habit, nature and the often odd behaviour of their fellows – that's not to say that some names were probably totally irrelevant and were just meant to offend! For example: Curst Eckie, Ill Will Armstrong, Fingerless Will Nixon, Ill-drowned Geordie Nixon, 'Dog Pyntle' Archie Elliot and 'Buggerback' George Elliot, not to mention Nebless Clem Croser.

With names like Winking Will, Gleed John, Jock with the Lippe, Fat Collope, Sore John, Lang Will, Little Hobbie, Fair Archie, Foule Thowngs, John wi' the jak, Wide hoise, Whyte Serk, Rede sleeves, Fire the Braes, David-na-guid-priest, Flie the Gaist, Farley the Plumpe, Crak Speare, Fat Sow, Crat, Scabbit, Shag, Half-lugs, Unhappy Anthon, Hob the King, David the Lady, Out-with-the-Sword and Prikit-up Archie, it is not difficult to imagine the appearance, style and demeanour of these men as a motley band of dangerous ruffians.

The Tools of Reiving

The most important piece of equipment the Reiver owned was his horse. These small, agile, sure-footed Galloway ponies were well trained in the art of crossing difficult and boggy terrain in the dark in all weathers where others would fear to tread. These valuable animals were the ideal all-purpose mount and served admirably as fast transport for day-to-day raiding and as a war horse for light cavalry. They could cover tremendous distances over rough country and claims of between 70 and 150 miles a day have been made, although it is generally believed that between 60 and 80 miles a day would have been quite possible. These animals were not only cheap to buy, but they were also reasonably easy to look after – there is evidence to suggest they did not need shoeing, took little or no grooming and after a day's, or night's, riding were simply turned out to pasture.

The secret, of course, was the speed at which the Border lords or heidman could rally riders – the Bold Buccleuch, for instance, could raise over 2,000 horsemen, ready for action, at short notice.

Naturally such an important possession as a horse of this quality was bound to attract legislation, and the Scots, who were prolific breeders of quality animals, were making an enormous amount of money by selling to the English. However, in the second half of the 16th century, fearing short supply, the Scots government banned the sale of any horses to the English, and by the late 1500s the sale of any English horses to the Scots was also strictly prohibited because animals were in short supply. These laws, however, were not followed and a healthy, if illicit, trade in animals continued in both directions.

Once he was mounted on his horse

the Borderer was an impressive sight. In the early days he wore a simple steel cap or sallet on his head, but this was later replaced by the light and open burgonet or Steil Bonnet – these helmets offered maximum protection while not restricting vision. They were usually peaked with cheek plates and flared to the base of the rear to protect the neck, often lined with leather, and they were regularly polished with animal fat to prevent rusting. By Elizabethan times these helmets were gradually replaced by the morion, which had a curved brim and a high comb – the better quality examples were raised from one piece of metal – a stern test for the blacksmith. The Reiver might possibly wear a mail coat over his linen or wool shirt, but more traditionally it would be a jack or jak – a coat of thick strong leather with metal plates sewn into the quilting to provide extra protection. It was cheaper to make and lighter than plate armour but was just as effective against the slashes and thrusts from the enemy. Backs and Breasts of steel were also worn, but only by the more wealthy Borderers who had to suffer the inconvenience of carrying extra weight.

Long leather boots over thick breeches would complete the clothing, although in times of war men would need to be identified and would tie a kerchief around their upper arms and have either a St George's Cross or St Andrew's Cross sewn on to their jaks.

Throughout the 1500s the longbow was still popular as an effective weapon and was especially favoured by the infantry soldiers, but increasingly towards the end of the century the Border Riders, although they did indeed use the bow, started to carry firearms – the arquebus, the caliver or, more usually, the dag or heavy handgun.

Border foot soldiers usually used the bill – or a local weapon called the Jedburgh Axe – a deadly combination of a pike and a cleaver.

The Border Riders also carried swords and daggers. Basket hilted swords were favoured – particularly back swords which were used with a downward stroke – either hilt first, to smash into an enemy head or face or blade with a vicious downward cutting slash. Small round shields were also carried to protect the rider from returned blows. The Reivers favourite weapon, however, was the lance – it was over 12ft long and could be used either couched (under the arm) for charges or for throwing.

The Border Reiver, thus equipped, was ready to either ride out on a raid or into battle – either way he was a formidable enemy.

The Market Cross, Ancrum

In the village of Ancrum, just north of Jedburgh, the market cross stands on the triangular village green. It was Bishop Blackadder of Glasgow who, in 1490, established a regular market here in a failed attempt to turn the village into an important centre of trade and commerce.

It was also from the market cross that the March warden would have a horn sounded and proclamations read announcing the names of those who had, for one reason or another, been made 'broken men' or had been 'blown out', or declared outlaws.

The Capon Tree - Jedburgh

To the south of Jedburgh in a small field, just before the bridge opposite the entrance to Ferniehirst Castle, is the Capon Tree. This magnificent oak tree is thought to be one of the last surviving trees of the ancient Jed Forest and is estimated to be in excess of 500 years old.

It has great connections with the days of the Border Reivers – this is where the famous 'Jeddart Justice' was administered to those habitual law breakers rounded up in the area. 'Jeddart Justice' was part of King James's 'Pacification of the Borders' – suspected miscreants would be hanged first and their trial would follow directly. The name derives

The Capon Tree.

from the practice of nailing the caps of those executed to the branches – hence 'Cap On Tree'.

Reiving and Raiding

In 1586 William Camden, the noted historian, describes how he observed Border Riders spearing salmon in the Solway Firth: 'The district nourisheth a War-like kind of men, who have been infamous for Robberies and Depredations, for they dwell upon the Solway Firth, a fordable Arm of the Sea at Low Waters through which they made many times out-rodes into England for to fetch in Booties, and in which the inhabitants on both sides with pleasant pastime and delightful sight hunt Salmons of which there is an abundance.'

This reference to the riders' great skill must have inspired Sir Walter Scott, who gives a vivid account of this incredible skill in his novel, *Red Gauntlet (Letter IV)*.

Reiver presentation ~ Tullie House Museum

Tullie House Museum in Carlisle offers a splendid audio visual presentation that captures the mood and atmosphere of the Reiver days in the Borders. The museum also offers the opportunity for historical research through its award-winning facilities.

Camden's contemporary, John Lesley, Bishop of Ross has also written about the Reivers, providing what is perhaps the best, and certainly the most quoted, contemporary account of reiving – this account is so atmospheric it prompted Reiver expert George Macdonald Fraser, in *The Steel Bonnets*, to hint that the good Bishop had perhaps had more experience with reiving than he was telling!

He describes what was possibly a long-distance foray that could have been mounted by a small band of

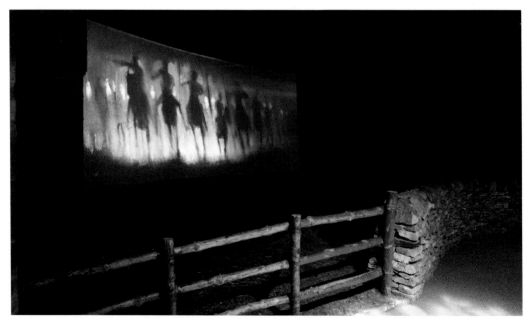

Border Reiver presentation, Tullie House Museum.

riders, perhaps from Liddesdale, moving deep into the English Middle March, with the need for silence and stealth being of absolute importance.

This is possibly the nearest thing to a first-hand account and gives an understanding of what it was like to be a reiver of either side.

'They sally out of their own borders, in the night, in troops, through unfrequented by-ways, and many intricate windings. All the day time, they refresh themselves and their horses, in lurking holes they had pitched upon before, till they arrive in the dark at those places they have a design upon. As soon as they have seized upon the booty, they, in like manner, return home in the night, through blind ways and fetching many a compass. The more skilful any captain is to pass through those wild deserts, crooked turnings and deep precipices, in the thickest mists and darkness, his reputation is the greater, and he is looked upon as a man of excellent head.

And they are so very cunning that they seldom have their booty taken from them…unless sometimes, when, by the help of bloodhounds following exactly upon the tract, they may chance to fall into the hands of their adversaries. When being taken they have so much persuasive eloquence, and so many smooth insinuating words at their command, that if they do move their judges, nay, and even their adversaries (notwithstanding the severity of their natures), to have mercy, yet they incite them to admiration and compassion.'

Although reiving took place throughout the year, it was mainly between Michaelmas (29 September) and Candlemass (2 February) when most of the damage was done. At this time of year the cattle were in good condition after summer feeding, the days were shorter, providing more cover of darkness, and as often as not there would be a ground frost which, of course, made the animals easier to drive across the wild country.

The Muckle Toon Bell ~ Carlisle

The Muckle Toon Bell was cast in about 1400 and was rung whenever raiders were sighted approaching the city. By the 1700s it was used to chime the hours in the Old Town Hall Clock; however, in 1880 a fire swept through the Town Hall roof and the excessive heat caused the bell to crack down one side and it could no longer be rung.

Today it is on display in the keep of Carlisle Castle.

The Muckle Toon Bell, Carlisle.

The first action in mounting a raid was for the riders to gather at a pre-arranged rendezvous. Each surname had its own designated tryst place known to all its members. It was possibly an area on an open moor marked by a cairn of stones or could have been a well-known landmark. Sir Walter Scott tells of a place near Linton, at the foot of the Cheviot Hills, known as The Tryst, where a circle of stones enclosed an area of short smooth turf where the leader of a raid would have cut his name along with directions for latecomers to follow the foray.

Raids varied in size, but the average number would be anywhere between 12 and 50 riders. Sometimes great forays with over 2,000 lances would be launched with the object of sacking of a small town or village, or perhaps even several small towns, while at the other extreme it might be a matter of just a couple of men looking to lift two or three head of cattle or a few sheep. The distances covered varied enormously and there are records of raids as far north as the outskirts of Edinburgh and as far south as North Yorkshire. During the night was the favourite time to mount a raid – preferably by moonlight, although some raiders preferred those nights with no moon as it provided more cover. The technique of the foray depended largely on the number of riders involved. Obviously to small bands stealth and secrecy were of the utmost importance, while large-scale raids could, and had to, travel more openly knowing that they had enough men to deal with any confrontation other than a well-equipped army.

Theeves Roads

Many cross border tracks and routes became well used and well worn – these were under constant observation by watches or the warden's men. Some leaders of reiver bands relied on being able to pick their way through treacherous bogs and mosses – even in the dark.

Tradition has it that raids were often mounted along the many established routes of 'Reivers or Theeves Roads' which can still be traced on the map; however, it seems more likely that each leader of a raid, who would be, by reputation, a master of his dubious craft, would have his own secret routes across the more remote wastes, windswept moors and wild hills.

Even after successful negotiation of the treacherous bogs and mosses and finding their way through the dark and, possibly, the bad weather, the Reivers still did not have things their own way. By the mid-1500s Lord Wharton, who by reputation was a tough March warden, had established a system of watches that were in place by day and night along the whole length of the border, on hilltops, at fords or in each valley, to give early warning of any raids. Each local heidman or landowner was responsible for maintaining a mounted and armed

Bogs and mosses were difficult to cross.

band of men ready for immediate action – it was estimated that over 1,000 men were needed on watch at any one time. Severe punishments were inflicted for the neglect of duty, and failure to resist a raid carried the death penalty, although this punishment was eventually reduced to being held responsible for the value of goods stolen. In addition to the normal watch, 'plump watches' of extra strength could be mounted when needed and there was also support by small, fast mobile patrols which could be rushed to any point at short notice.

To help the defence even further, particularly on the English side, packs of 'slewedoggs' were kept which could be unleashed to track raiders on the hot trod. An early warning system of beacons was also essential to give notice of impending raids. These networks were operated from Carlisle Castle on the English side of the border and from Home Castle on the Scottish side. The beacons were sited on hillsides about 600 or 700ft high within easy access of a watchman who could race to raise the alarm. These hill beacons were later supplemented by heavy metal baskets on the roof of every tower and castle. Once the alarm was raised, lights would appear across the hills and on the towers and people were quickly alerted to an impending raid.

Plaque – Carlisle Castle

On the wall of what was the Governor's or Elizabethan range there is a replica of a stone plaque, an example found on no other outside wall of any other castle in the country. It shows the date of 1577 and the coat of arms of Elizabeth I quartered with those of France – 'the lion trampling the fair lilies down' – and records that the queen erected this work at her own expense while Lord Scrope was warden of the English West March.

The scale of raiding was enormous – absolutely colossal. The *Calendar of Border Papers* – two thick volumes running to almost 2,000 pages – is a catalogue of complaints against the families and individuals who maintained this dreadful reign of terror and fear. The entries of livestock 'lifted', 'insight' (household goods) stolen, homes burned and men and

Opposite: Mosses were a combination of bogs, dense scrub woodland and trees.

The plaque, Carlisle Castle.

women wounded, kidnapped or even killed are almost endless. Reiving was a constant and almost inevitable threat that must have been hell to live with, not only every day but also for years on end. The following are typical examples of complaints from the *Calendar of Border Papers*, which serve to illustrate the magnitude and depth of the raiding.

One man, simply referred to as Sowerby, who lived near Coldbeck had his house broken into and suffered the most cruel treatment: 'They set him on his bare buttocks upon a hote iron, and they burned him with a hote girdle about his bellie and sundry other parts of his body to make him give up his money, which they took, under £4.00.'

This complaint was lodged on Martinmas 1587:

'The poor widow and inhabitants of the town of Temman complain upon the laird of Mangerton, laird of Whithaugh, and their complices; for the murder of John Tweddle, Willie Tweddle, and Davie Bell, the taking and carrying away of John Thirlway, John Bell of Clowsegill, David Bell, Philip Tweddle, Rowye, Carrock, Thomas Allison, George Lynock, and Archie Armstrong, ransoming (or putting them to ransom) as prisoners; and the taking of 100 kine and oxen, spoil of houses, writings, money and insight, (value) £400.00 sterling.'

Dickie of Dryhope, another of the notorious Armstrongs, along with over 100 of his men, kept up the family rciving tradition by attacking Hobbie Noble's village, driving off over 200 head of cattle after destroying nine houses and burning Hobbie's son, John, alive, along with his pregnant wife.

An entry from 1590 gives excellent detail of stolen goods, on this occasion by the Elliots:

'John Forster of Heathpole, servant to Sir John Forster; complains upon John Ellott of the Hewghehouse, Clement Croser, Martin's Clemye, John Croser, 'Eddies John', Gib Foster of Fowleshields & to the number of 30, who stole six oxen, 6 kye, 4 young nowt, ane horse £10, a nag 40s, a sword 13s 4d, a steil cap 10s, a dagger and knives 4s, 2 spears 6s 8d, 2 dublets 12s, 2 pair breches 8s, a cloak 5s, a jerkyne 2s 6d, a women's kertle and a paire of sleves 10s, 9 kerchers 18s, 7 railes 7s, 7 partletts 7s, 5 paire line sheites 27s, 2 coverletts 10s, 2 lynne sherts 7s, a purs and 6s in monie, a womans purs and 2 silke rybbons 2s, a windinge cloth 6s, a featherbed 8s, a cawdron 13s 4d, a panne 2s 6d, 4 bonde of hemp 2s 8d, a paire of wooll cards 20d, 4 childrens coates 8s, 3 sherts 3s: on 3rd November last.[sic]'

And yet, one of the sobering thoughts about Border reiving is that no one thought of the actual pillaging or theft of another's goods on a foray as a particularly great crime. To the Reivers, it was a tradition that was handed down through the generations and the difference between reiving with its traditional blackmail, kidnapping, feud killing and other 'crimes' was quite distinct, illustrated perhaps by an

incident in the early 1600s which made important and unusual news in a Border report when two highwaymen were arrested, tried and hanged in Newcastle for their crimes.

Ponteland Pele Tower

Ponteland, north of Newcastle, marks an ancient crossing point on the River Pont, and it was here in 1244 that a peace treaty between England and Scotland was negotiated. The village is positioned on the well-trampled path taken by raiding Scots – they burned the castle here and took the Lord of the Manor prisoner on their way from Newcastle to Otterburn. The tower was attached to the vicarage and provided speedy and convenient refuge in times of danger. A pele tower was simple in construction but extremely strong. Walls over 10ft thick and a heavily-reinforced door meant the defenders could hold out against vastly superior numbers and the building was impregnable to anything short of artillery bombardment. A determined force, however, could eventually overcome this strong defence by either breaking in through the roof or by 'Scumfishing'; the practice of breaking down the door and filling the bottom floor with material that would burn easily and smoulder for several hours – this would smoke out the defenders with stifling heat.

The Union of the Crowns

During the final years of the reign of Queen Elizabeth I, the Reivers and their activities had almost got out of control.

Disorder was so widespread that the only course of action open to the wardens was to set one group of villains against the other.

On the 24 March 1603 Queen Elizabeth died, and with her passing a new era was to dawn on the Borders. However, the Reivers thought that Law and Order was automatically suspended at the death of a monarch and took advantage of the situation by mounting a huge raid into the West March. This became known as Ill Week, and in a fury of raiding activity over 4,000 head of cattle and about 5,000 sheep and goats were lifted. The Earl of Cumberland blamed the Grahams for the uprising, although Armstrongs, Elliots, Nixons and Crosers had also been heavily involved.

James VI of Scotland travelled south to take the English Crown, making him King of both nations – and therefore there would be no need for a frontier.

Soon after he was crowned he did away with the marches, abolished the post of warden and changed the name of the Borders to 'The Middle Shires'. His next step was to set up a commission of five Englishmen and five Scotsmen to administer the law. James decreed that, 'All rebels and disorderly persons will be prosecuted with fire and sword...'

Their first job was to order all the strongholds to be demolished, and about 40 of these belonging to the Elliots were destroyed; however, some of the others escaped unharmed – their solution to these was to rule that all their yetts should be made into ploughshares. All the inhabitants were instructed to destroy their armour and weapons, and it became an offence to keep a horse valued at more than 50 shillings. Furthermore, the Border laws were abolished and everyone had to obey the Law of the Land. One of the things that this stated was that 'if any Englishman stole in Scotland or any Scotsman stole in England any goods to the value of 12d he shall be punished by death'. The Pacification of the Borders had begun. Offenders were swiftly rounded up and dealt with quickly by what came to be known as 'Jeddart Justice' – from the number of Reivers who were justified at Jedburgh – many without proper trial. The appointment of Sir George Home, Earl of Dunbar, in 1606 to take charge of the pacification speeded up the process, and he rounded up many notable Reiver leaders including Armstrong of Mangerton and Martin Elliot. By 1611 he had executed over 230 important Reiver leaders.

Lord William Howard of Naworth Castle, or Belted Will as he was widely known because of the striking baldric he wore, joined in with the job of pacification with great enthusiasm, exceeded only by that of, surprisingly, the Bold Buccleuch, who had been one of the greatest haters of the English that the Borders had ever seen. He met with another noted leader, Walter Scott of Harden, at Jedburgh to discuss how best to put a stop to all the violence and robbery, no doubt causing a few raised

eyebrows considering their past records.

Several families were singled out for special treatment: the Grahams, for instance. Many were executed out of hand, while others were deported to the more remote parts of Ireland. The Armstrongs of Whithaugh suffered a similar fate and many of those were sent to Ireland in 1609 as part of a plan to settle Ulster to re-enforce the protestant population. Many Reivers drifted back from Ireland only to find that their lands had been given to the Scotts and the Elliots.

Old habits die hard, and small bands of 'Moss Troopers' still roamed the countryside, making a living by lifting what cattle or sheep they could and stealing horses in one country to sell on the other side of the border. Violence, however, persisted and there are references during the 17th and 18th centuries to the uncouth and unsettling nature of the Borderer.

Eventually the mists of time closed around them all, but the ghosts and spirit of these great riding clans of the border of England and Scotland live on in the family names and the unique character of the people who live in the border area today.

The Riding Families of the Border Marches

Archbold
Armstrong
Beattie
Bell
Burns
Carleton
Carlisle
Carnaby
Carr
Carruthers
Chamberlain
Charlton
Collingwood
Crisp
Croser
Crozier

Cuthbert
Dacre
Davison
Dixon
Dodd
Douglas
Dunne
Elliot
Fenwick
Forster
Graham
Gray
Hall
Harden
Hedley
Henderson

Heron
Hetherington
Hume
Irvine
Irving
Johnstone
Kerr
Laidlaw
Liddle
Lowther
Little
Maxwell
Milburn
Moffat
Musgrove
Nixon

Noble
Ogle
Oliver
Percy
Potts
Pringle
Radcliffe
Reade
Ridley
Robson
Routledge
Rutherford
Salkeld
Scott
Selby
Shaftoe

Storey
Simpson
Tailor
Tait
Trotter
Turnbull
Wake
Watson
Wilson
Woodrington
Yarrow
Young

The Percy Lion and Alnwick Castle.

Border History

Alnwick Castle, Northumberland

Alnwick Castle has been at the centre of conflict between England and Scotland for hundreds of years. During his rampage through Northern England in 1297, William Wallace launched a savage attack on the castle which was successfully defended by Sir William de Vesci, whose family had owned it since the 1100s. However, when he died he left no legitimate heir and the estate was placed in the care of Antony Bek, Prince Bishop of Durham, to be held in trust for his illegitimate son, William de Vesci of Kildare. Many historians believe that the unscrupulous Bek did a shady deal and sold the estate to Lord Percy in 1309 – however, there are just about an equal number who think that Bek did nothing wrong. Due to the lack of any documentary evidence, the truth is shrouded in mystery – the problem was further compounded by the fact that when William de Vesci of Kildare was killed at Bannockburn his heirs laid claim to Alnwick and had to be paid a substantial cash settlement instead.

Alnwick Castle became the Percy stronghold, but it was after the coronation of Richard II in 1377 when Percy was created 1st Earl of Northumberland that the family came to their full prominence as prodigious warriors and clever statesmen. The 1st Earl was the father of the famous Harry Hotspur, the charismatic leader of the people who was immortalised by William Shakespeare in his play *Henry IV*. The 1st Earl and his son strengthened the fortifications of the castle – their duties as wardens of the English East March meant they had to protect the unstable border area from the incursions of the reiving

Scots. The Scottish Douglases were their traditional enemies, and it was probably the Battle of Otterburn that was the most memorable confrontation. Although the Scots won the battle, their leader, the Earl of Douglas, was killed and both Harry Hotspur and his brother Ralph were taken prisoner and subsequently ransomed for a substantial figure. The Percys took their revenge at the Battle of Homildon Hill, near Wooler, in 1402. However, it was after this battle that they became involved in a heated dispute with the king over prisoners' ransom money – each thought it was due to them. And, even though the Percys had helped Henry V gain the throne, they entered into a plot with Edward Mortimer, and the Welsh patriot, Owen Glyndwr, to remove the king from the throne. They even entered an alliance with 'the auld enemy' – the Scots – and

marched south to join up with the rest of the rebels, but Henry intercepted them at Shrewsbury.

Harry Hotspur was killed in the subsequent battle, but his uncle and Douglas, the Scots leader, were taken prisoner. It was a disaster that was to haunt the family for years.

The 1st Earl was pardoned by the king within six months, but, failing to learn his lesson, he revolted again in 1405 in league with another of his kinsmen, the Archbishop of York. This uprising also ended in catastrophe, when at the Battle of Shipton Moor, the archbishop was taken prisoner and executed, but the earl escaped and remained at large until 1408 when he was killed in the defeat in the Battle of Barnham Moor, near Tadcaster. As an example to all traitors his severed head was stuck on a spike on the

Alnwick Castle.

middle tower of London Bridge and his body was quartered and sent to 'the four corners' of his northern lands.

After being fortunate enough to have their estates restored to the family yet again the Percys went on to fight in the Wars of the Roses supporting the Lancastrians. The 3rd Earl was killed at Towton where it is said that 38,000 men lost their lives in what is thought to have been England's bloodiest battle.

The 4th Earl was involved in the famous Battle of Bosworth Field – he started out on the side of Richard III, but when things started to go wrong he switched to that of Henry VII – for whom he eventually became a tax collector. Even then things did not work out well because while he was carrying out this unpopular task, near Thirsk in Yorkshire, he was attacked by a mob and killed.

The 5th Earl was the one who was entrusted with providing a protective escort for the young Princess Margaret, Henry VII's daughter, during her journey north to marry James IV of Scotland.

The 6th Earl was all ready to marry Anne Boleyn when Cardinal Wolsey intervened and she was stolen from him to become the second wife of Henry VIII. Although extremely distressed, the earl eventually married the Earl of Shrewsbury's daughter, but he died without leaving a direct heir and the estate passed to a nephew.

From then on the family fortunes took a downturn.

The 7th Earl was executed for his involvement in 'The Rising of the North', and his successor, who was also suspected of being an ardent supporter of Mary, Queen of

Scots, died in the Tower of London in rather unusual and suspicious circumstances.

The Percies continued the tradition of upsetting the monarch when the 9th Earl was mixed up in the ill-fated 'Gunpowder Plot' in 1605; he was fined £20,000 and made to swear that he would never return north again.

Arthuret Church, Longtown

Arthuret Church stands on the outskirts of Longtown overlooking Solway Moss. The original church on the site, served by the monks of Jedburgh, dated from 1150 but was ruined in the cross-border violence of the 14th and 15th centuries. The church is sited right on the edge of the Debateable Land – the centre of reiving for the West Marches.

Richie Graham used the porch of Arthuret Church as a place to collect his 'blackmeale' or blackmail – he even kept a register of those who had paid, or perhaps, more to the point, those who had not. The word blackmail was used in its original sense because it was in the Borders that the term was first used. Rent was usually known as 'mail' – greenmail was paid out as rent for grazing land, whitemail was rent paid to the landlord but blackmail was paid to the Reiver. It was, in effect, protection money. It was the Grahams who developed this, from merely opportunism, into a thriving business and any unfortunate who could not, or would not, pay either in money or in kind would suffer the dreadful consequences. His stock would be taken and his house and insight burned. However, the offence was

Arthuret Church, Longtown.

A Graham family gravestone.

difficult to control and the law was not much help – according to Scottish law, in the mid-1500s the non-payment of blackmail carried the death penalty, but by the end of the century things had improved a little and the payers were only fined, while the takers were punished at the discretion of the March warden. It was only in the early 1600s that the extortion of blackmail was made a capital offence in England. Blackmail is one of the words that has passed into the English language from the Reivers, along with bereaved, botched and sackless.

The present Arthuret Church dates from 1609 and is dedicated to St Michael and All Angels. It was built on the orders of James I, the newly-crowned King of England. The finance was raised by public subscription through a collection organised by the Archbishop of Canterbury after the king had received reports of the local people being without faith, virtue or regard for any religion. The building of the church was,

therefore, a significant gesture by King James as part of his 'Pacification of the Borders', and the Gothic style of architecture served to emphasise religious stability, particularly as Protestant reformation was being firmly established throughout the kingdom. The tower was completed by 1690, and its design echoes the style of the strongly fortified border pele towers of the preceding centuries.

Archie Armstrong, the court jester to James I and his son Charles I, is buried near the ancient cross in the churchyard. Interestingly, this is thought to have been erected by the Knights of Malta in the 14th or 15th century. Archie was buried on April Fool's Day 1672. The status of court jester was greatly elevated by the early Stuart kings, and Archie's position was, in effect, gentleman groom of the chambers as well as a jester. He had the ear of the king and part of his income came from bribes given by those who would like him to arrange an audience

Archie Armstrong is buried somewhere near this Maltese Cross.

Askerton Castle, Gilsland

Askerton Castle was one of a line of strongholds stretching eastwards from the Solway Firth that defended the English West March – Rockcliffe, Burgh-by-Sands, Scaleby, Askerton, Naworth and Bewcastle. These, combined with the natural barrier of the broad River Eden, the deadly Solway tides and, of course, the mighty Castle at Carlisle, made sure that the English Middle March presented a more appealing target.

Askerton stands in a remote but valuable position at the edge of the fells between Gilsland and Bewcastle. News of any raid that looked serious could be quickly despatched to Naworth or Carlisle, but those affairs of a less urgent nature could be handled by the land-sergeant, who was stationed here with a strong garrison.

Thomas Carleton must have enjoyed his position as land-sergeant here in the 16th century because when the office was offered to John Musgrave he refused to leave. Of course, it could have been because the Carletons had no time for the Musgraves and a feud between the two families was constantly simmering. In fact, it was suspected that Carleton was behind an attempt to murder Musgrave by several Grahams; when they failed to shoot him they tried to burn him alive by setting fire to the house where he was staying.

Henry II originally granted Askerton Manor to Sir Hubert de Vaux in 1157, and it was his son who founded Lanercost Priory. Askerton passed to the de Moulton family by marriage and thence to Sir Ranulf Dacre who married Margaret, the last of the de Moultons. It then passed to his descendent

with the king. Archie enjoyed great favour, he was granted a patent to produce tobacco pipes and was made a freeman of the city of Aberdeen. However, an inappropriate remark made about Archbishop Laud of Canterbury saw Armstrong disgraced at court: Archie was asked to say grace, and he burst forth with 'All praise to God, and little Laud to the de'il!' However, in spite of his transgression he was lucky enough to be allowed to return to Arthuret to retire.

Archie had always been sharp of wit, and this is illustrated by one of his own stories: in the days before he was court jester, when he lived on the banks of the River Esk, he stole a neighbour's sheep to replenish his larder. He had just killed the sheep and was about to skin it when he saw his neighbour approaching the house. Archie quickly looked around for somewhere to hide the carcass and spotted the cradle in the corner. He stuffed the sheep into the cradle and covered it up. When the owner came into the house, Archie protested his innocence and furthermore swore an oath that if ever he took anything from his neighbour's sheep folds he should be condemned to eat the flesh that the cradle holds.

Askerton Castle.

*Askerton Castle on
the edge of
Bewcastle Waste.*

Opposite: Aydon Castle courtyard.

Thomas Dacre, who was criticised for his part in the Battle of Flodden, but who did extensive fortification work on Naworth, Drumbrugh and, of course, Askerton.

The last Dacre heir died prematurely in the late 1560s and the estate came, by marriage, into the hands of Thomas Howard, Duke of Norfolk. His dishonesty got the better of him, and he was executed in 1572 by Elizabeth I for his part in the crisis caused by Mary, Queen of Scots, when he became a likely candidate for her hand in marriage. However, his son, the highly regarded Lord William, who married Elizabeth Dacre, lived a long and happy life at Naworth.

Eventually the estate passed into the family of the 9th Earl of Carlisle, who are the present owners.

Aydon Castle, Corbridge

Aydon Castle, Corbridge.

Aydon Castle or 'Aydon Halle', as it was called in the 13th and 14th centuries, occupies an excellent position above the well-wooded dene of the Cor Burn. It is possibly one of the finest examples of a fortified manor house in the country. It was built in the late 1200s by Robert de Raymes, a wealthy Suffolk landowner who married Maud Wortley, a member of the Heron family of Ford Castle. In 1305 he was granted a licence to fortify his house by Edward I, and although it was not in immediate danger this soon appeared to be a well anticipated course of action. Within a couple of years Edward I died and the Scots, under Robert the Bruce, took full advantage of their victory at Bannockburn and turned their attention to northern England. A Raid in 1311 followed by a bigger raid in 1312 saw the land around Corbridge devastated and laid to waste, with looting and burning. Fortunately, Aydon's defences had held during these Scottish incursions, but in 1315 Robert the Bruce and his army returned and made a more determined effort. Hugh de Gales had been left in command of Aydon by the absent Robert de Rames on this occasion, but in spite of it being well supplied and equipped he negotiated a surrender with the Scots with the result that the castle was

Aydon Castle.

Aydon Castle.

Opposite: Jock's leap, Aydon Castle

trade. He became Sheriff of Northumberland and served as an MP. After his death he was succeeded by his three sons; the most successful of these was Nicholas, the youngest. He seemed to be continually in trouble over money and served a term in prison when he was involved in the murder of John Coupland, a royal official. However, de Raymes had powerful friends, among them Henry Percy, Earl of Northumberland. With the help of the Percys he held a series of important government positions and eventually managed to arrange the marriage of his daughter to the powerful and influential Sir Robert Ogle.

In the following two centuries things went into decline for Aydon and for the de Raymes family, and by 1450 it was described as a 'ruinous castle'. By the early 16th century the castle was occupied by tenants such as the Shaftoes, and eventually Aydon was made over to Sir Reynold Carnaby, who was building up a large estate centred around Hexham.

On two occasions Border Reivers are mentioned in connection with Aydon. One incident took place early in 1386 when a band of English and Scottish Reivers captured a man from Aydon and carried him off over the border and held him to ransom.

The other involves a local legend: it tells of how two Reivers were captured during a raid on Aydon. The usual punishment for anyone being caught red handed was immediate execution. It was decided that these two should have their throats cut and be thrown from the roof into the Cor Burn far below. One of the protagonists escaped this dreadful fate by taking a huge, almost superhuman,

ransacked and burned. The Scots continued to create havoc in Northumberland and any law and order collapsed, and in 1317 Hugh de Gales and a band of rebels took back Aydon, but this time he pillaged and burned the place. Next to attack Aydon was an army led by King David II of Scotland in 1346, on his way to the Battle of Nevilles Cross near Durham. The occupants prudently surrendered in return for their lives, but the castle was burned again. In 1347 Robert de Raymes's son – also Robert – took over Aydon and he restored the family living through the wool

leap across the ravine to safety – the place where this is alleged to have happened is remembered in the name 'Jock's leap'.

The Battle of Ancrum Moor – 12 February 1534

Shortly after the Battle of Solway Moss, King James V died when he was only 30 years of age. His daughter Queen Mary was only a year old and Scotland would be ruled by the Earl of Arran as Regent – this only served to further emphasise the great unrest within the country. King Henry VIII tried to unify the two kingdoms by suggesting the marriage of Queen Mary to his own son, Prince Edward – however, this situation was not only complicated by religious difficulties between

the two countries but also the differences within Scotland. Negotiations failed and Henry responded with what has become known as 'The Rough Wooing'. In May 1544 the English landed at The Firth of Forth, immediately laid to waste the town of Leith, and then burned Edinburgh – it is said the flames could be seen for miles and miles – a grim warning to the Scots, who were already in turmoil with the internal unrest their country was suffering. Later that same year the English Army under the ruthless command of Sir Ralph Euer, warden of the English Middle March, and Sir Brian Laiton, the Governor of Norham, ravaged the Borders with devastating brutality – effectively leaving much of the area under English control. To further their own good about 750 Scottish Reivers from Liddesdale

Ancrum Moor.

and Teviotdale, along with several other Border lairds, joined forces with the English, who numbered just over 5,000 – including 3,000 foreign mercenaries and a further 1,200 Borderers.

The king had promised Euer great reward for all the plunder taken and land captured; this encouraged him to pursue his campaign with brutal and greedy enthusiasm. He drove his army ever onward, destroying Melrose and its Abbey – callously destroying the Douglas tombs – yet another act calculated to insult and infuriate the Scots who could do nothing more than mount small raids of resistance against the enemy flanks.

It was Archibald Douglas, 6th Earl of Angus and Lieutenant of the Border, who had assembled a local Scottish force to attempt to stop the English – but more and more men volunteered now that a respected Scottish leader had emerged – they were also joined by the Earl of Arran and his lances,

bringing their numbers up to nearly 1,200 soldiers.

The English Army started the journey back to its headquarters in Jedburgh but, perhaps because the men were weighed down with plunder and brimming with over-confidence gained from their easy success, they set up camp on Ancrum Moor.

The English saw a small number of Scots on the horizon, who immediately turned away in apparent retreat – the English Cavalry followed in hot pursuit, well ahead of their foot soldiers, a mistake which was to cost them dearly. The cavalry reached the ridge but were blinded by the setting sun – disorientated, they were attacked by the full Scottish force in battle formation. The Scots pressed forward their attack and the English fell back in retreat. The 750 Reivers on the English side took note of the progress of the battle and switched sides to the Scots. Seeing this, the English troops then broke and fled –

a pursuit followed with wholesale slaughter – both Euers and Laiton were killed and, as the story goes, their bodies mutilated.

The battle was watched with great interest by the local people who, when they saw the English were routed, joined in the massacre with whichever weapon they could bring to hand. Earlier, the English had burned the Tower of Broomhill, killing the old lady, her family and servants who lived there – this further fuelled the desire for revenge and the locals set about the English with the same disregard for mercy.

There is a story attached to the event that tells of a beautiful young woman named Lilliard who went to the battle with her lover – he was killed and she picked up his sword and continued to wield it in the bloody conflict against the hated English, sustaining grievous wounds, until she herself was cut down. She is remembered by a monument on Lilliards Edge, on the site of the battle, that describes her part in the fray:

> Fair Maiden Lilliard
> Lies under this stane
> Little was her stature
> But muckle was her fame
> Upon the English loons
> She laid monie thumps
> An' whwn her legs were cuttit off
> She fought upon her stumps.

After the Scottish victory the English border regions were placed in readiness for a huge Scottish incursion which never came – the Regent was unwilling to risk a major invasion.

As an angry consequence of the battle, King Henry sent another army, this time into Scotland, with over 12,000 men under the command of the Earl of Hertford, to continue the devastation and despoliation of the country – over 300 towns and villages were destroyed, along with the Border abbeys of Dryburgh, Kelso, Jedburgh and Melrose – huge areas of land were laid to waste and many men, women and children were put to the sword.

Perhaps the best memorial to the battle is another inscription on Lilliard's Stone:

> And long all who that day fought
> And wreaths of honour won
> Live in their country's heart and thought
> For deeds heroic done
> And tell each succeeding age
> How valiant hearts may battle rage
> And foil a tyrants armoured bands
> Who grasps at power with blood-stained hands.

The Battle of Flodden Field

Early in the summer of 1513 James IV of Scotland made the fatal decision to invade England. The official reason was to avenge the death of Sir Robert Kerr, warden of the Eastern March, who was killed in a brawl involving one of the Herons of Ford Castle. However, some historians have suggested that it was because James was unhappy with the dowry he received on his marriage to Margaret Tudor, although another well-known legend tells how the Queen of France sent James her glove, accompanied by a love letter, urging him to attack England to ease the military pressure on her own country.

James gathered an army that has been estimated at between 60,000 and 100,000 men and marched south, crossing the Tweed at Coldstream, destroying the castles of Wark, Norham and Etal in his path before making his headquarters at Ford Castle. The English needed a little time to respond, and it took them 18 days to gather an army between the time James crossed the border and the battle itself. While James dallied at Ford Castle, occupied, it is said, with the charms of the young and attractive Lady Heron, some of his army left, reducing his number of men to around 30,000. Meanwhile, Thomas Howard, the Earl of Surrey, commanding on behalf of Henry VIII, had landed archers at Tynemouth and marched them to meet the forces of Northumberland under the Percys and the army of Thomas Ruthall, Bishop of Durham, commanded by Sir William Bulmer.

In all, Surrey assembled an army of some 30,000 men just west of Alnwick before marching to Wooler Haugh, where he made his headquarters. James had taken up a strong position on Flodden Hill. Surrey divided his forces, sending the vanguard and artillery, under the command of his eldest son, Edmund Howard, to cross the Till by Twizell Bridge, circling the Scottish position. Surrey himself took the infantry and cavalry across the fords between Etal and Ford. James remained in position on his hilltop. Only when the English forces were re-united and making their way to the adjacent Branxton Hill did James take action.

At 4pm on 9 September 1513 – a day to be henceforth known as Black Friday – he set his tents ablaze and, under cover of the smoke, charged downhill to engage the English. He had allowed an almost unassailable position to be outflanked and rendered useless –

Flodden Field.

however, he had the flower of Scottish nobility under his command and a great victory was still a possibility.

Edmund Howard was in command of the English right flank, and his men were first to take the powerful Scottish onslaught. His line wavered but did not yield – it was strengthened by a tough contingent of Border Reivers under the command of Lord Dacre. The Scots regrouped to attack again and might have easily crushed the English flank and turned the field, but a strange thing happened – they simply disappeared! Tradition has it that they found looting more profitable than fighting, and of course these men were also Reivers under the command of Lord Home.

Possibly the best and the worst sides of the Reivers' character came out at Flodden, and there are many conflicting stories about their part in the battle. Surrey commented about the Scottish Borderers that 'they were the boldest and the hottest I ever saw of any nation'. But Home is reported to have said that the man who did well that day was the man who stood and saved himself.

Home and Dacre were heavily criticised after the battle and were accused of collusion

Flodden Field monument.

in order to minimise casualties. They denied it, of course, but bearing in mind the Borderers' cynical attitude to national allegiance it could possibly have been true, although the real truth will never really be known.

The battle ebbed to and fro for hours, until Sir Edmund Stanley and his men outflanked the Highlanders, wheeled and charged downhill into the back of the Scottish Royal Division. The end was now in sight; in fact, by nightfall it was all over. James himself is said to have died bravely, cut off and surrounded by only a handful of his men. The dawn of the next day revealed the truth: Scotland's military might was no more. At least 10,000 men lay dead on the field, although some English eye-witness accounts put the numbers as high as 15,000 or even 17,000.

The English lost 1,700 men, including five knights and 10 squires. The worst blow for Scotland, however, was the loss of almost the entire nobility, gentry and ruling class – among the dead were an archbishop, a bishop, 10 earls, 19 barons and masters, the Provost of Edinburgh and over 300 knights, lords and gentlemen.

As well as a whole generation of nobility, entire companies of shire and burgh levies had been wiped out, such as the men of Selkirk, of whom only one, a pikeman named Fletcher, returned to tell the tale.

During the night, after the battle, the Reivers, in their traditional style, pillaged the bodies of the dead while the English Reivers also plundered the tents and the baggage and removed several horses belonging to the English Army. One English officer is quoted as saying that 'the Borderers did full ill'. The Bishop of Durham was particularly aggrieved and complained bitterly that they had removed some of the prisoners and ransomed them back to the Scots – and that they had done more damage to the English

Army than the Scots. He also went on to say the English Borderers were 'falser' than the Scots and that his men were more worried about the English Reivers than they were about the Scots.

King James's body was identified by Lord Dacre and was laid in the 12th-century church at Branxton, from whence it was taken to Berwick and from there to London. It remained unburied until the reign of Queen Elizabeth. The head was hacked from the body for 'sport' but was eventually claimed as a souvenir by the queen's glazier, who had it buried in an unmarked grave at St Michael's, Cornhill, in London.

The sombre granite cross is said to mark the spot on the battlefield where King James fell, but the Scottish lament 'The Flowers of the Forest' is perhaps the most emotive reminder of this awful Scottish tragedy:

'We'll hear nae mair lilting at our ewe milking
Women and bairns are heartless and wae
Sighing and moaning on ilka green loaning
The flowers of the forest are a' wede away.'

Revenge had been taken for Bannockburn, but once the battle was over Surrey disbanded his army and left the affairs of the Borders to be managed in the traditional manner by the enthusiastic Lord Dacre. He ordered huge raids to be mounted into the Scottish West and Middle Marches. There is evidence that in one raid more than 4,000 head of cattle plus horses and insight were taken and that the area was left 'burning from daybreak to late afternoon'.

There was a certain amount of retaliation by the Scots, but it could not match the English attacks. Liddesdale, Esksdale and Teviotdale were all but devastated, and Dacre boasted that all was quiet from Bowness to the Hanging Stone – there had never been so much robbery and raiding in Scotland, and he added that he hoped it would continue.

The Battle of Halidon Hill

The Battle of Halidon Hill was fought on 19 July 1333; however, there were several events in the preceding years that contributed to it. In 1318 Robert the Bruce captured Berwick – it was a traitorous sentry on the 'Kow Gate' who allowed entry to the Scots. In 1328 Edward III renounced any claim on Scotland in return for £20,000, paid by the Scots as compensation for any damage done to England. Later that same year Joan de Terribus, Edward's sister, married David, son of Robert the Bruce – great hopes for the future depended on this union and earned the princess the name of 'Make Peace', but it was not to be. When Robert the Bruce died, Edward III invaded Scotland and laid siege to Berwick on 12 April 1333. However, the town was well prepared. Realising he could be in for a long siege, Edward took a large army of men further into Scotland, laid waste to the Borders and captured Edinburgh Castle. Meanwhile, Lord Archibald Douglas brought his army to relieve Berwick, and in an attempt to lure the English away he laid siege to Bamburgh Castle. The plan did not work as Bamburgh was strong enough to hold off a siege as long as necessary.

By 15 July the town of Berwick agreed a surrender in five days hence, and Sir Alexander Seton, the deputy governor, agreed for his eldest son Thomas to be held as a

Halidon Hill, looking towards Berwick.

hostage. Seton's youngest son was already being held by the English and Edward, fearing that the town may be relieved before the five days were up, demanded immediate surrender, threatening to execute Seton's sons if it was not forthcoming.

It is recorded that Sir Alexander would have agreed to the terms but was dissuaded by his mother – and both of the sons were put to death in view of their parents on a small hill still known as 'Hang-a-Dyke-Neuk'. There is a record of two skulls, reputed to be those of Seton's sons, being on display in the poor house in Tweedmouth in 1873.

Lord Archibald Douglas returned from his unsuccessful siege of Bamburgh and decided to engage the English in battle. His troops crossed the Tweed and found the English Army firmly established on Halidon Hill, about two miles to the north of Berwick.

It is said that prior to the battle a challenge

to single combat was issued by a gigantic Scottish ruffian called Turnbull, who hailed from that notorious family of Reivers from West Teviotdale, associates of the Olivers, the Trumbles and the Rutherfords.

Turnbull advanced boldly, accompanied by a huge mastiff war-dog. The challenge was taken up by a Norfolk knight called Sir Robert Benhale. The growling Mastiff, with dripping jaws, suddenly launched a ferocious attack on the knight, who deftly side stepped the dog's attack and with one mighty blow cut the enormous beast in half. Turnbull moved quickly forward into the attack, but Benhale cleverly avoided the fierce blows aimed at him with amazing agility, and with great dexterity he turned and lopped off Turnbull's left hand and, before he could react, swiftly cut off his head.

The battle began with the Scottish Army advancing up the hill, but it would be the

English archers who would once again prove their superiority. They showered the close Scottish ranks with a rain of arrows, followed by a powerful advance by the spearmen and Men at Arms. The Scots Army, unable to stand the tremendous onslaught, fled in disarray and panic. Thousands of Scots, including their illustrious commander, lay dead on the Battlefield. Halidon Hill became known as one of the greatest military disasters in Scottish history and Berwick immediately surrendered.

The Battle of Otterburn

The battle which made the village of Otterburn famous was fought on 19 August 1388 and is memorable for being fought by moonlight. There is some dispute as to whether the site of the battlefield is on the east or west side of the Otter Burn, although it is popularly believed to have taken place between Fawdon Hill and the small valley to the north which runs down to the route of the present A68.

Prior to the advance into England by the Scots, an interesting incident took place in the Church at Southdean (pronounced Souden) not far from the border line at Carter Bar. The leaders of the Scottish Army were assembled in this church in 1388 to plan their foray into England. Unknown to them, an English squire had got into the church and overheard all their secret plans. After he had gleaned sufficient information he slipped out of the church, planning to hurry back to England with his news. Unfortunately he found that his horse had been stolen, and he was faced with a difficult situation: if he reported his horse stolen he would give away

his cover, but if he left on foot he would be questioned as a gentlemen on foot dressed for riding would certainly attract attention. His fears were justified, and he was soon caught and brought before the council of leaders. Under interrogation he was forced to reveal his identity and all that he knew about the position and condition of the English forces. It is said by some historians that under pressure he became a double agent, but unfortunately there is no record of his career from that day.

The following incursion by the Scots was a result of James, Earl of Douglas, taking advantage of the information gleaned and of the weak government of Richard II. He gathered an army of about 4,000 hand-picked men and mounted a stealthy lightning strike through Northumberland and penetrated as far as Brancepeth in County Durham, leaving a wake of devastation, pillaging and plundering. On their return they camped for three days outside the walls of Newcastle, which was defended by an army under the command of Sir Henry and Sir Ralph Percy, sons of the Duke of Northumberland. There were several skirmishes and it was after one of these that Sir Henry (the celebrated 'Harry Hotspur') challenged Douglas to single combat in front of the wooden barriers constructed to defend the New Gate.

Hotspur was unhorsed and lost his spear with its silken pennant to the victorious Douglas, who held it aloft exclaiming that he would take it back to Scotland and display it as a trophy. Hotspur threatened that he would never get it out of Northumberland. The challenge was laid down.

Early the next morning the Scots struck camp and marched to Ponteland, which they

Southdean Church.

*Percy's Cross,
Otterburn.*

burnt after capturing and firing the castle. They then marched to Otterburn, where they attacked the tower, this time without success. The Scots camped in the nearby valley with the intention of returning home the next day.

Meanwhile, Sir Henry Percy, eager to make good his threat, had left Newcastle with about 14,000 men and had arrived at Otterburn under the light of the full moon. With the impulsiveness that had earned him the name of 'Hotspur', he launched an attack on the enemy even though his men were weary after the long march. The English broke into the Scots' camp but mistakenly their attack was directed against servants and camp followers – allowing precious time for the Scottish troops to manoeuvre around the hillside and attack the English flanks.

It seemed at first that the superior numbers of the English would be victorious, but soon the tide was turned, and although the Earl of Douglas was killed the Scots pressed home their advantage and a complete rout ensued. Henry and Ralph Percy were both taken prisoner and the fugitives were chased five miles from the scene of the battle.

The Bishop of Durham had raised an army with the intention of helping the Northumbrians, but not far from Newcastle they met some of the fugitives who carried word of the disastrous battle. His army were panic stricken by the news, and the bishop was forced to return to Newcastle as his troops were unable to control their fear. He made an indignant and patriotic appeal to the knights and squires of the town, with the result that the next morning he set out for Otterburn at sunrise with 10,000 men under his command. His army stopped short of the enemy, who knew of their arrival. The Scots

then blew their hunting horns and made such a noise that a contemporary account says 'That it seemed as if all the devils in hell had come hither to join in the noise, so that those of the English who had never before heard such were very much frightened'.

In spite of this the bishop did advance further, but seeing how well the Scots had chosen and fortified their camp he decided not to risk an attack and led his hastily gathered and ill disciplined army back to Newcastle. Another tactical mistake by the English side.

The Scots then returned across the border. The bodies of the Earl of Douglas, Sir Robert Hunt and Sir Simeon Glendinning were all buried in Melrose Abbey. Hotspur, as the price of his ransom, paid for the building of the Castle of Penoon for his captor, Lord Montgomery. Sir Ralph Percy and several other knights were allowed to remain in Northumberland until their wounds healed, but they were then required to either give themselves up to the Scots or to pay the amount of their ransoms.

The spot where the Earl of Douglas fell is marked by a stone pillar about 15ft high on a circular pedestal of rough stone. Percy's Cross, as it is mis-named, stands in a small plantation of fir trees about ¾ of a mile to the north of the village. The battle is further remembered in two ballads, one English and one Scottish; each differs in their respective narratives, which may perhaps be accounted for on patriotic grounds!

Berwick-upon-Tweed

Towards the end of the 13th century Berwick-upon-Tweed was probably one of the

Berwick Castle.

wealthiest cities in Scotland and an important centre of commerce and administration. It was here in 1291 that Edward I presided over a great gathering of English and Scottish noblemen to consider the rival claims of Bruce and Baliol to the Crown of Scotland. Edward declared the decision in favour of John Baliol, who swore an oath of allegiance to the English Monarch. In 1296, because of certain grievances, Baliol broke into open rebellion and invaded Northumberland. In his fury Edward advanced north to inflict a terrible vengeance and the first blow fell on Berwick. A combined attack by land and sea overwhelmed the town. Edward himself, mounted on horseback, was the first to leap the dike – his soldiers, inspired by their king's actions, carried all before them. All the horrors of war were unleashed on a rich, well

Berwick Castle and the Royal Border Bridge.

Berwick Castle, near the railway station.

Cumberland Bastion, Berwick Elizabethan Town Walls.

populated, commercial town ravaged by a savage unstoppable army led by a commander thirsty for vengeance. It is said that 17,000 men, women and children were put to the sword – reputedly the streets of the town ran red with blood for two days – the churches, in which many of the inhabitants had sought sanctuary, were defiled with blood, spoiled of their sacred artefacts and used as stables by the English Cavalry. This ruthless massacre caused a sensation all over the country, especially in the Borders where it had much to do in creating the feeling of bitter hostility with which the English were regarded ever after. Edward had lit the fuse.

He ordered the building of new walls to defend the town, although much of the construction was still going on during the reign of Edward II and, indeed, they were further strengthened by Robert the Bruce in 1320. When they were finished they stood 22ft in height and had 19 defensive towers and five gates in their 2½ mile length.

In spite of the new walls, there were still revolts and uprisings. To harass and despoil the English was looked upon as an almost sacred duty and first William Wallace took up the challenge and then Bruce the Younger,

Elizabethan Town Walls, Berwick.

grandson of the original claimant to the throne. In 1312 a stealthy move by Bruce to take the town was thwarted by a barking dog, and he had to wait another six years for success.

It was in Berwick that a barbaric punishment was inflicted on the Countess of Buchan who had crowned Bruce at Scone. She was imprisoned for four years in the castle and suspended from one of the towers in an iron cage, which exposed her to the scorn, mockery and abuse of all passers by.

Berwick has had an eventful history, and its people have witnessed many desperate and shocking events in the Borders. Many kings, and queens have passed through the town on their way to great victory, miserable defeat, or in sheer bloody retribution. Edward II fled to Berwick after his humiliating defeat at Bannockburn, and about 20 years later Edward III's longbowmen inflicted a devastating and satisfying revenge on the Scots at Halidon Hill.

In 1377 a band of desperate Reivers, apparently only eight in number, crept into the castle at night, murdered the governor, Sir Robert Boynton, and overcame the garrison. They were joined by about 40 of their associates and succeeded in holding the castle for eight days against 7,000 English archers and 3,000 cavalry.

Eventually artillery was beginning to dominate warfare, and to combat this Mary I engaged the famous military engineer Sir Richard Lee to improve Berwick's defences. However, most of the work on the new walls was completed during the reign of Elizabeth I – the Reivers in this part of the Borders had taken to skirmishing with the English soldiers on a regular basis, and the extra fortifications would no doubt reduce any chance of success they were having during their incursions. The Elizabethan Walls were constructed within the Edwardian Walls and took over 20 years to complete. They were the most expensive project that was undertaken during the reign

King James Bridge, Berwick.

of Queen Elizabeth I, costing almost £130,000.

James VI of Scotland, on his way to being crowned James I of England, experienced a perilous crossing of the rickety wooden bridge built by Henry VII. Although he was a shrewd and cunning man, he was reputed to be a bit of a physical coward, and he was seized with abject fear and panic when he crossed the bridge. He flung himself off his horse onto the planking and called upon Almighty God to save him. He was half

carried, crying and screaming, to the other side where he sank to his knees and kissed the ground. He is reputed to have said 'What a shoogly brig! Is there ne'er a man in Berwick whae can werk stane to mak a brig o'er the Tweed?'

A new bridge was built in 1611, but it was not ready for use until 1626 and finally finished in 1634 at a cost of £16,000.

This stone King James Bridge is anything but shoogly.

Bewcastle, Cumbria

The gaunt ruin of Bewcastle Castle dates from about 1092. It was one of three built along the border by William II to protect Cumberland from Scottish attack; the other two were Carlisle and Brough. It followed a well-established tradition in the area – the castle was built from stones obtained by robbing the remains of a roman fort which had once occupied the site. In the 1300s the castle was owned by the de Swineburns, one of whom married John de Strivelyn, who was appointed Constable of Edinburgh Castle and also became a Member of Parliament.

By the 1400s Bewcastle Castle had passed into the ownership of the de Middletons, during whose ownership it was captured by the Scots. The de Middletons were eventually ransomed and shortly afterwards moved to their less remote home in Belsay Castle.

In 1478 the castle was taken over by Richard, Duke of Gloucester, when he was warden of the English West March. In 1493 he granted the position of Constable of Bewcastle to the Musgrove family. Indeed it was Thomas Musgrove, when he was constable in the latter days of reiving times, who, commenting on the ruinous state of the building, lamented that 'there is hardly a room where a man may sit dry'. Official positions in the area were filled by the Salkelds, the Lowthers, the Carletons, the Musgraves and the Dacres – although sometimes it was difficult to tell whose side they were on. Another wry comment by Thomas Musgrave sums up the situation: 'They are a people that will be Scottish when

Bewcastle Castle.

Bewcastle Waste.

they will and English at their pleasure'. However, when Musgrave lost the Constable's position at Bewcastle to William, Lord Dacre, it is said that he stole all the lead and broke all the windows in a fit of anger – fuelled, no doubt, by the fact that the Musgraves and the Dacres were at feud for the best part of 300 years.

The Musgraves were restored to position by 1531 and continued to protect the area – seemingly locked in a constant struggle to repel raids by the Armstrongs of Liddesdale. A large attack mounted by the Armstrongs and their associates, led by Lord Maxwell, warden of the Scottish West March, saw extensive damage inflicted on the castle, the surrounding buildings and the barmkin. Reivers made good use of the green track leading through the Bewcastle Waste – this had been the Roman Maiden Way – their road from Birdoswald.

This was such a popular route for raiders it was referred to in old documents as 'a

common passage well known to the thieves of Tynedale, Bewcastle and Gilsland as well as the thieves of Liddesdale'. With ever his eye on the Reivers' story, Sir Walter Scott's 'Guy

St Cuthbert's Church, Bewcastle.

Mannering' has a scene where Dandie Dinmont is riding his nagge, Dumple, over Bewcastle Waste and is attacked by footpads.

It is probably safe to say that at some time nearly every able-bodied man in Bewcastle was involved in reiving. Even the local vicar was drawn in, despite the fact that the church is next door to the castle. His name appears on a list of complaints made by the Scots against the English in 1552 – it mentions the Grahams, particularly George of the Gingles, plus Will Patrick, priest of Bewcastle, helped by his curate John Nelson, when they lifted a substantial number of cattle on a raid.

By 1604 the castle was almost a ruin and eventually passed into the ownership of the Grahams of Netherby. Interestingly, a property company started a scheme to sell sectional shares of the castle to anyone who would buy them, particularly in America, but unfortunately the idea of owning part of a ruined castle on the edge of Bewcastle Waste had no appeal and the company and the idea, along with part of the castle, collapsed.

St Cuthbert's Church was built during the reign of Edward I, also using stones from the roman fort. However, it was rebuilt in the 1700s and the dedication changed to that of St Cuthbert. The Bewcastle Cross in the churchyard is of particular note and possibly dates from sometime around AD675, and the time of Benedict Biscop – it is inscribed with runes and enigmatic figures, providing much material for speculation, discussion and research. It is accepted to be, along with the Ruthwell Cross in Scotland, one of the finest examples of an Anglo-Saxon Cross in the whole of Europe.

Black Middens Bastle, near Bellingham, Northumberland

A few miles to the north west of Bellingham, almost at the confluence of the

Black Middens Bastle.

*Black Middens
Bastle.*

Tarset and Black Burns, stands Black Middens Bastle. A substantial 16th-century fortified farmhouse, it is one of a group of three, possibly four, bastles in the immediate vicinity. Nearby are the ruins of an 18th-century cottage which was possibly built on the ruins of an earlier bastle, while half a mile and a mile to the northwest are Shilla Hill and Bog Head bastle houses. The word bastle is derived from the French word bastille meaning fortified place. Shilla Hill is thought to have been the home of 'Hodge Corbit' or 'Corbit Jack', and Bog Head, or possibly Black Middens, was where 'Barty o'the Comb', one of the well-known Milburn Clan, lived with his family. In addition to being a farmer, Barty Milburn also found supplementary benefit in doing a bit of reiving or lifting. He awoke one frosty autumn morning to find a party of stealthy marauding Scots had legged it with his sheep. Barty summoned his fellow family member Corbit Jack, who lived

nearby, and together they set off to avenge the theft. After a few miles the trail went cold – to the north of Carter Fell – and it looked like the pair would have to return

*Black Middens
Bastle.*

home empty handed, until Barty had the bright idea to lift someone else's sheep as replacements.

Things were going well until they reached Chattlehope Spout when two large, angry Scots – the rightful owners of the sheep – caught up with them. Obviously, a fast and furious, vicious fight broke out at the top of the waterfall. Jack was killed and Barty took a deep gash to the thigh. Fuelled by heated anger, Barty swung his sword as hard as he could at Jack's killer and cut his head clean off: 'his heid sprang alang the heither like an inion!' The other Scot attempted to escape, but he too was cut down. Barty took the Scots' swords and other possessions and lifted Jack's body onto his back. In spite of being badly wounded, he drove the stolen sheep safely home, making a detour to leave Jack's body at his own door.

'Barty o' the Comb' was typical of the hard men who lived in those days of the Border Reivers – everyday life was an accepted cycle of raid and reprisal.

Brackenhill Tower, Longtown

Brackenhill Tower at Longtown, near Carlisle, is an excellent example of a fortified Border tower house and is strategically sited between two deep ravines in the heart of Reiver country on the border of the Debatable Land and Bewcastle Waste. Architectural experts say that it is unique in that it is built in the Scottish style but on English soil. It was built in the mid-1500s and is strongly associated with the Graham family. It is thought that Fergus Graham of Mote originally purchased the house from Sir Thomas Dacre and gave it to his son,

Richard, or Richie, as he was better known, and it was he who built the main tower house in 1584.

Richie Graham was a powerful and feared Borderer – his notoriety even spread to the court of King James in London. It is widely thought that Richie was the reason the king singled out the Grahams for intense persecution during his 'Pacification of the Borders'.

Richie Graham could put 500 men in the saddle at any one time, such was his influence and following, but his reputation, and indeed that of the rest of the Graham family, was less than savoury and the *Calendar of Border Papers* lists about 60 Grahams as outlaws. They were wanted for murder, robbery and blackmail; one complaint stated that 'they had despoiled a dozen Cumbrian villages, sheltered felons, fought the warden's men, extorted money from their enemies and burned the house of Hutcheon Hetherington to force him into the open so they could cut him into collops [slices]'.

Opposite:
Brackenhill Tower.

Brackenhill Tower.

St Michael's Church, Burgh-by-Sands.

St Michael's Church, Burgh-by-Sands

St Michael's Church in Burgh-by-Sands is built completely within the area of the Roman Fort of Aballua on Hadrian's Wall. It is thought that it stands on the site of one of the main buildings – the headquarters or possibly the granary – and, of course, very conveniently the fort offered a ready-made supply of dressed building stone. The church actually received its dedication in the 12th century, but the actual construction date is not known. However, it is safe to say that it is built largely in the Norman style, with much restoration dating from the 1800s.

However, the western tower was built in

The iron yett, St Michael's Church, Burgh-by-Sands.

the 14th century. Edward I died at Burgh-by-Sands on 7 July 1307, and this event marked the point in time from which there was constant unrest, trouble, skirmish and war between England and Scotland. The border is a large area and was therefore very difficult to defend. The effect during the 14th century was that personal defence was a priority, with the result that defensive farmhouses and towers were built all over the area. A popular method of defence in rural areas was the fortification of church towers, and there are three excellent surviving examples in Cumbria, particularly St Michael's in Brugh-by-Sands and others at Newton Arlosh and Great Salkeld.

The western tower of St Michael's was originally intended to be used as a belfry, but also had to double as a place of refuge and safety in times of trouble. It has walls about 7ft thick with no access door from the outside, only arrow slits on the ground floor and very small windows on the first floor. There is no arch opening into the tower from the nave, only a very small doorway guarded by a strong, iron gate or yett. During raids and incursions by Scottish Reivers the priest and his villagers would feel secure in the safety of this well-defended building, and of course they could ring the bells to attract attention and hopefully get help to relieve their awful plight.

Caerlaverock Castle, Dumfries

Caerlaverock Castle was built in 1277 by Sir Herbert Maxwell. Edward I invaded Scotland in 1296 and Caerlaverock Castle,

Caerlaverock Castle.

which was regarded as one of the main strategic strongholds to the south west of Scotland, was caught up in the war. Many of the Scots swore their allegiance to Edward, including Sir Herbert Maxwell and his son John. However, because of Edward's unfair and dominating interference in Scottish politics many of the Scots began to resist. Edward increased the intensity of his incursions, directing his fury at Galloway in general and at Caerlaverock in particular. Although it was not one of the most significant operations in the Scottish War, it is perhaps one of the best known incidents because it was so accurately recorded. The English Army numbered over 3,000, commanded by almost 90 knights; the castle was defended by Robert de Cunningham with only 60 men – the Maxwells were not in the castle during the siege. The English brought siege engines from Lochmaben, Roxburgh and Carlisle. De Cunningham's small force surrendered after two days, and the English were greatly surprised at how many men had held them off – the records say that about half of the Scots were hanged from the castle walls and the others were allowed to go free. The castle remained in the possession of the English under the control of Sir Eustace Maxwell, who had been appointed keeper.

However, not long after his appointment he changed sides again to support Robert the Bruce. He was besieged in his castle by his former masters but held out for a few weeks, until he was ordered to demolish it by Robert the Bruce in case the English wanted to use it. Eustace changed sides yet again when Edward Baliol was crowned king in 1322; the Maxwells were supporters of the Baliols. He

Opposite and left: Caerlaverock Castle.

repaired Caerlaverock and defended it for Edward.

By the 15th century the Maxwells still held Caerlaverock, and it was at this time that Herbert Maxwell was created Lord Maxwell and the second Lord Maxwell, Robert, was made warden of the Scottish West March.

Tragically four of the Maxwells were killed at the Battle of Flodden Field in 1513, but by 1536 Robert, the Fifth Lord, had become Regent of Scotland and the family controlled the three castles that were the key to the Scottish West March – Threave, Lochmaben and, of course, Caerlaverock. James V stayed in the castle prior to the Battle of Solway Moss, and not only did the Scots lose the battle but Sir Robert Maxwell was taken prisoner and ransomed.

He suffered the same fate again in 1544 when the English captured the castle, although it was retaken in 1545, but by 1570 it was back under English control, taken by the Earl of Sussex.

The Maxwells had always been devout Catholics, even after the Reformation in 1560. Robert Maxwell went to Spain to help arrange the Armada invasion and on his return attempted to rally support for it. He was arrested and put in prison, and 22 of his kinsmen were executed, but Maxwell himself managed to escape punishment, although he had to pay for his treachery by surrendering all of his castles to the Crown. By 1592 he was back in the Borders, all his wrong-doing forgiven, and reinstated as March warden.

At the Union of the Crowns in 1603 the Maxwells still held Caerlaverock, but in 1640 Robert, the Earl of Nithsdale, surrendered it to the Covenanters Army after a two-week siege.

The castle eventually passed to the Herries family, related to the Maxwells by marriage, and thence to the Dukes of Norfolk, and in 1946 it was transferred into the care of the state and since then into the care of Historic Scotland.

Carlisle Castle

The City of Carlisle has always been one of the main routes into England and as such needed to be well defended. It was William Rufus who first established a fortification there when he regained possession of Cumberland from Malcolm of Scotland. His castle was almost certainly a wooden tower on a mound surrounded by a defensive ditch. Eventually, of course, it was replaced by a fortress built of stone, which became the focus of special attention from the Scots, but with no success – the castle was so strong that it remained impregnable for five and a half centuries.

Edward I made Carlisle Castle his base for his Hammering of the Scots towards the end of the 13th century, and it was here that he held a parliament with all the due ceremony that would continue as an English tradition. After his death, Edward's son was proclaimed king here and received the homage of his nobles.

The gatehouse and keep, Carlisle Castle.

The most determined attempt to take Carlisle was made by Robert the Bruce in 1315; he used every weapon in his armoury, including a new siege engine, and every tactic he knew, but the constant wet weather was against him and the garrison held firm – they only lost two men. The unsuccessful Scots left after 11 days, but not before they had trampled the surrounding cornfields and driven off all the cattle.

In 1327 Edward II was deposed and murdered. His captors treated him badly and tried to starve him, but he did not die until they thrust a marrow bone into his rectum and plunged a red hot poker through it, and his outwardly unmarked body was displayed for public scrutiny. But his son, Edward III, was a much more accomplished soldier, and he learned and sharpened his battle skills against the Scots then applied this experience to great effect against the French. In 1346 the English had decisive victories at the Battle of Crécy and the Battle of Neville's Cross in Durham, where King David was taken prisoner. After this no invading English Army ever occupied Scotland again. With the king's attention on the French Crown, Carlisle Castle became less important nationally but more important in regional affairs. It became the headquarters for the wardens of the English West March, and it was for this purpose that the castle's outer gatehouse was built in 1383.

The Scots laid siege to Carlisle again in 1385 but were driven back by the newly-installed cannon mounted on the keep. By the late 1400s the castle was given a purpose-built gun tower – Richard of Gloucester's tile tower in the south-east curtain wall – and it incorporated gunports in the lower levels to

The keep, Carlisle Castle.

command the lower slopes and was constructed from brick, then a new material, favoured for defensive works.

Carvings in the walls on the second floor of the keep, reputedly done with an iron nail, are said to have been done by Richard's prisoners. In the basement dungeon is the 'Licking Stone', which attracted moisture from the air. It was used by prisoners in an attempt to satisfy their thirst, and their tongues have worn a deep hollow in it.

By the early 1500s Henry VIII had appointed Thomas Howard, Duke of Norfolk, to Carlisle, and he recommended

Richard of Gloucester's tile tower, Carlisle Castle.

Cannon, Carlisle Castle.

that it should be further repaired and its armoury strengthened, although the engineer and builder he employed, Stefan von Haschenperg, was accused of 'spending a lot of money to no purpose'.

Scottish Guns, captured at the Battle of Solway Moss in November 1542, were included in the armoury of the castle, already well supplied with ordnance; however, in 1547 a huge explosion in the magazine left some huge cracks in the walls of the keep. Fortunately Queen Elizabeth ordered the fortress to be repaired and strengthened.

In 1568 Mary, Queen of Scots was brought

The Licking Stone, Carlisle Castle.

from Cockermouth and held prisoner for two months until she was found more secure accommodation in Bolton Castle.

In 1596 the castle was the setting for possibly the most dramatic and stirring episode in Reiver history – the rescue of Kinmont Willie Armstrong by the Bold Buccleuch, the Keeper of Liddesdale. In the aftermath a furious Queen Elizabeth demanded the surrender of Buccleuch. He appeared before her and she demanded to know how he had dared to carry out such an audacious raid. To which he replied 'Madam, what would a man not dare to do!' The queen was impressed by his reply and, full of admiration, she is reputed to have cried 'By God! With 10 such men our brother of Scotland might shake the firmest throne in Europe!' After the death of Elizabeth in 1603, James VI of Scotland succeeded as James I of England and history would dictate that Carlisle Castle's role as an important Border fort would be renewed.

Carlisle Cathedral.

Carlisle Cathedral

The position of Carlisle as a prominent border city is reflected in its dramatic and turbulent history, but in its beautiful cathedral is a contrast – it is a haven of beauty and peace – but has still witnessed many dramatic events.

In the south wall arcade of the building is the carving of a head which is thought to be that of King Edward I. It was here in 1297 that he received the allegiance of Robert the Bruce, sworn on the sword that was said to have killed Thomas Beckett. The sword which had belonged to Hugh de Morville, a Cumbrian knight, had become an object of great veneration.

The Becket Sword.

Edward I, Carlisle Cathedral.

Cartington Castle, Rothbury

The remains of Cartington Castle lie just to the north west of Rothbury, a couple of miles along the Thropton to Callaly road. It stands on private land but the nearby footpath affords an excellent view. The castle was mentioned in the list of Border forts drawn up in 1416, but permission to crenellate was not granted until 1441. In reality it was a fortified house rather than a castle but is described in the 1542 summary as 'a fortress of two strong towers and other storage houses and kept in good repair'.

The 15th-century Prior's Tower was commissioned by Prior Senhouse and serves as a reminder of those dangerous Border days when even the clergy had to be constantly vigilant, and indeed prepared, in case of surprise raid or attack.

A great occasion in the history of the castle took place on 16 November 1515 when it was visited by Princess Margaret, the sister of Henry VIII and the wife of the Earl of Angus. She had travelled from Harbottle

Cartington Castle.

Castle where she had given birth to a daughter, Lady Margaret, who was to become the grandmother of James I, and through whom he was to claim the English Throne. Unfortunately she was very ill when she was moved and could not bear horses pulling the litter and so it had to be carried by Lord Dacre's servants. When she was sufficiently recovered she was moved from Cartington to Brinkburn Priory and then onto Morpeth.

One of the more famous owners of the castle was Sir Roger Widdrington who, in his capacity of deputy warden of the March under Sir Robert Carey, distinguished himself to the notice of Queen Elizabeth.

Cessford Castle, Morebattle

Cessford Castle occupies an imposing position on the northern edge of the Cheviot Hills, about halfway between Morebattle and Crailing. The site is easily defendable and has a wide outlook, particularly to the north and east. The castle, or Border tower as it is perhaps more accurately described, stands almost at the crossing point of two ancient trackways; one crosses Bowmont Water and leads up over Cocklaw and the other is the old Roman Road of Dere Street – this was the green road by which the Scots, carrying the body of the dead Douglas on a bier of branches, returned from the Battle of Otterburn.

Cessford Castle enjoyed a formidable reputation in the early days – the Earl of Surrey said it was one of the strongest fortresses in the Borders.

About 100 years ago a workman digging near the north wall unearthed a sword and a dagger – the basket hilted sword was richly decorated with silver and over 40 inches long; the dagger measured just over 24 inches in length and was engraved on the blade with a Scottish thistle and a crown. These valuable artefacts provided much food for thought and speculation.

Andrew Kerr was given the barony of Cessford by the Earl of Douglas in 1446 and a later member of the family, Robert, held the position of warden of the Scottish Middle March in the late 1500s – he must have been ruthless in the execution of his duty because he was attacked and killed by three Englishmen – but only one of these escaped to brag 'that he had pulled the Scottish lion's tail'.

However, there have been Kerrs on the Scottish border since the 14th century and their notorious reputation has always encouraged trouble and even violence. They were also unpopular on their own side of the border and carried on a lengthy bitter feud with the Scotts of Buccleuch. On one occasion Kerr of Cessford joined forces with the English Lord Grey to mount a raid on Buccleuch's lands. After a wild foray into the town of Hawick and ravaging the countryside as far as then Ettrick and Yarrow Valleys, they set fire to Catslake Tower – the home of the dowager Lady Buccleuch, who perished in the flames. A couple of years later Sir Walter Scott, warden of the Scottish Middle March and an important member of the Buccleuchs, was stabbed to death in the middle of Edinburgh by a gang of Kerrs and their associates.

In revenge for this outrage, Sir Walter's widow had the whole of the Kerr family outlawed, and even though the sentence was

Cessford Castle.

Dally Castle.

eventually relaxed it was years before those guilty of the actual crime returned to their homes.

Eventually the feud ended in an unexpected and romantic way. The Buccleuchs eventually demanded that Kerr of Cessford should go to St Giles' Church in Edinburgh and beg on his knees for pardon for the crime and, as a final penance, the rest of the Kerr family should agree to a peaceful settlement to the feud.

It was only Kerr of Ferniehirst who would not agree to the terms until Janet Scott, who was Buccleuch's sister, tried her persuasive powers. Where threat, argument and violence had failed, Janet's charms succeeded, and the two fell in love and were married, ensuring peace between these two feuding families.

Dally Castle, near Bellingham, Northumberland

The remains of Dally Castle stand on a small hill on the north bank of the Chirdon Burn, a small tributary of the North Tyne. It serves as a significant reminder of those days when North Tynedale was a part of Scotland. David de Lindsay built what was essentially a fortified house on the Chirdon estate,

granted to him by Alexander III of Scotland's sister. However, the king soon encouraged him to strengthen the construction, heighten the walkways and add battlements and corner towers. This did not go unnoticed, and Sir Hugh de Belboc, Keeper of Northumberland, pointed out to his king that it was built with such great strength that it would serve as an excellent base for any Scots harbouring sinister designs on Northumberland. It has been suggested by some historians that this was indeed the intent, and that both Wallace and Bruce made use of it when they mounted their devastating raids into Northern England.

A local legend tells of a subterranean passage that connects Dally Castle with Tarset Castle, only about a mile away, and that a carriage can be heard rumbling its way through the dark, bursting from the end to reveal the full horror: it is drawn by four black, headless horses driven furiously by a headless coachman, who could not see where he was going.

By the 1700s Dally Castle had fallen into ruin and by 1800 its stonework had been plundered to build the nearby Dally Castle House and Dally Mill.

The Devil's Beeftub – Moffat

Almost at the northern limit of the Scottish Marches, about five miles to the north of the attractive town of Moffat, the A701 road to Edinburgh climbs tortuously over the high wild Border hills – almost at the summit the ground to the east of the road plunges dramatically into a remote, steep, high-sided valley – this is 'The Devil's Beef Tub' – traditionally thought to be a place for hiding

Dally Castle.

stolen or 'lifted' cattle until the danger of discovery and punishment had passed, hence the name.

Standing on the high vantage point above the Devil's Beeftub, it is easy to imagine a band of Reivers with a herd of lifted cattle in a misty early morning – moving them out of sight into the safety of this narrow cleft in the wild hills.

This lonely site has also seen other dramatic incidents. In 1675 John Hunter, a covenanter, was shot by Douglases Dragoons in the hills above the valley.

A brave act by two mail-coach drivers is also remembered. In February 1831 the mail coach, travelling north to Edinburgh, became stranded in a dreadful blizzard. Unable to carry on the journey, the driver and the guard released the horses and tried to continue on horseback with the mail bags. The conditions were terrible and the two men died of exposure, but the horses made their way to a nearby farm. The alarm was raised but because of the awful weather it was five days before the men were found, still in possession of their mail sacks. A monument was erected at the viewpoint opposite the Beeftub to commemorate their devotion to duty.

Dryburgh Abbey, Melrose

Dryburgh Abbey is about four miles from Melrose. It originally belonged to the White Canons of the Premonstratensian Order who were brought to Dryburgh from Alnwick in Northumberland by Hugo de Morville in 1150. Although their rule was based on that of St Augustine, it was generally more strict, and it was supplemented with some of the more vigorous ideas from the Cistercian Order. They followed a hard way of life based on austerity and asceticism followed strictly to the devotion of God. The devotions and commitment were hard and this was emphasised by the fact that the whole abbey only had one fireplace for the monks to warm

Dryburgh Abbey.

Dryburgh Abbey.

Sir Walter Scott's tomb, Dryburgh Abbey.

themselves during the cold, hard Border winters.

Dryburgh is generally considered to be the most beautiful of the Border abbeys; it is situated on a loop formed by the River Tweed, surrounded by beautiful woodland, the richness of its now ruined buildings enhanced by the peace and tranquillity of the sylvan setting.

However, during the Wars of Independence with England, the abbey did not enjoy as peaceful a life as the setting would suggest. In 1322 King Edward II was camped nearby with his army – they were on their way back to England after another unsuccessful invasion attempt – when the sound of bells ringing in celebration attracted their attention. They attacked the abbey and burnt it to the ground.

Rebuilding began almost immediately. Robert the Bruce gave substantial financial help and this was supplemented by further grants and help from the Bishop of Glasgow.

A period of comparative peace which followed was brought to a sudden end when the abbey was attacked by Richard II in reprisal for Scottish raids carried out on the North of England – ' the Abbey Church was despoyled by hostile fyre'. Robert III followed the example of his predecessor and provided financial help for the rebuilding. This included giving the revenues of the Nunnery in Berwick-Upon-Tweed, which had just been closed because of the wayward behaviour of the Nuns. Many other helpful contributions were given by The Earl of Douglas, Lord Halyburton and Lord Maxwell of Caerlaverock Castle in Dumfriesshire.

Monastic life continued in spite of these difficulties and hardships, but unfortunately

there were signs that discipline was slipping and the abbot had to be granted special authority by Rome to deal with the problem. Their behaviour continued to get worse and the monks started to develop more appreciation of worldly possessions than religious devotions. This was leading to more and more cries for reform. To make matters worse, senior church appointments were being offered for their financial reward – particularly during the reigns of James IV (1488–1513) and James V (1513–1542). The system was being abused and many of the appointed officials, or commandators, hardly visited the abbey but still continued to draw their substantial incomes.

The abbey was raided again in 1522 by the Earl of Surrey, making more extensive repairs necessary.

In the autumn of 1544 the Earl of Hertford marched into Scotland with an army of over 12,000 men. Over 300 towns, villages, towers and churches were destroyed, along with the abbeys of Jedburgh, Kelso, Melrose and Dryburgh. Dryburgh never recovered from this dreadful, violent ravaging. It is now a peaceful and tranquil place that brings a gentle comfort and relaxation to the mind, and its beauty and mood have captivated people for over 200 years. And no wonder.

For many people the great association with Drybrugh is Sir Walter Scott. His favourite walk was around the abbey and his body is buried within its walls – a fitting resting place for a prodigious writer, a patriot and a great enthusiast for all things Scottish.

Edward I Monument – Burgh-by-Sands

Edward I died of the weakening effects of severe dysentery at Reedy Brugh Marsh, Brugh-by-Sands, on 7 July 1307 while leading

St Michael's Church, Burgh-by-Sands.

a campaign against Robert the Bruce and his Scottish Army. His body was laid in the nearby St Michael's Church, and he is remembered by a stained-glass window in the east wall. In 1685 a monument was erected in his honour by the Duke of Norfolk on the marsh where it is believed he died, but this was replaced in 1803 by the one seen today.

King Edward I – Longshanks – was a very strong, forceful personality and an imposing and dominating figure; at 6ft 2in he stood

Edward I Monument, Solway Firth.

head and shoulders above most other men of his time. He would not suffer fools gladly and his favourite method of overcoming problems was by turning to war – for which he seemed to have a remarkable talent. It would be the 17th century before any ruler of England would raise any armies larger that Edward did against the Scots or, indeed, the Welsh. And no other king made a greater effort to rule the whole of Britain – in only two campaigns he conquered Wales and reorganised Welsh Law and Government. That done, he made is eldest son (who was to become Edward II) the Prince of Wales, creating a tradition followed by every succeeding English monarch providing, of course, they had an eligible son.

The dispute over succession to the Scottish throne after the death of Margaret, Maid of Norway, in 1290 meant that Edward was drawn in to interfere in Scottish politics. There were 13 claimants to the throne, but they all recognised his power and agreed to abide by his decision. In 1292 Edward awarded the Crown to John Baliol, and in fact he probably had the best claim, but Edward refused to respect Baliol as a king and instead regarded him as if he were another English baron. This greatly angered the Scots and they turned to Philip IV of France for help, forming the treaty that would mark the beginning of 'the auld alliance' between the two countries. Edward was furious. In violent reprisal he sacked Berwick–upon-Tweed and inflicted further heavy defeat on the Scots at the Battle of Dunbar. In the rampage that followed he marched across Scotland as far as the Moray Firth. He captured many castles and removed such precious items as the Scottish Crown Jewels, Margaret's Black Rood, which was

supposed to contain part of the True Cross, and the Stone of Scone – on which all the kings of Scots had been crowned.

On 28 August 1296 Edward held a meeting in Berwick and over 2,000 of the most prominent Scottish landowners and church men were summoned and forced to sign and affix their seals to a series of documents swearing allegiance to Edward. These became known as 'The Ragman Rolls', and record such prominent Scots as Robert the Bruce, 6th Lord of Annandale, and his son the 2nd Earl of Carrick and Sir Reginald de Crauford, who was uncle to William Wallace.

In the south wall arcade in Carlisle Cathedral is the carving of a head, thought to be that of Edward I. It was here in 1297 that Robert the Bruce swore his allegiance to the English king on the Becket sword.

Due to a series of further emphatic victories, such as the Battle of Falkirk, by 1305 Edward thought he had gained control of Scotland and began its reorganisation under English administration. However, in 1306 Robert the Bruce made a bid for the throne with his involvement in the murder of John Comyn, Lord of Badenoch. Bruce was to lead his army against the English in the conflicts that would eventually see him take the Scottish Throne. Edward's reaction to Bruce was ferocious, and he brutally punished Bruce's supporters as if they were rebels. He would not regard them as soldiers, but this only added to further strengthen rather than weaken their patriotic attitude.

By the end of his reign the strain of the continual fighting on three fronts, against the French, the Scots and the Welsh, was beginning to have an effect on Edward's health, and when he died in 1307, at the age of 68, he was leading his army on yet another invasion of Scotland.

He did not trust his son's political judgement and fought violently with him on several occasions over these matters, and there is a record of him tearing out a handful of the young man's hair during one of these outbursts, but the fact remains that Edward I left a difficult legacy. The country was suffering under a heavy burden of debt and was engaged in a war against Scotland that could not be won.

However, his reign did leave a deep imprint on English government and society. His most enduring legacy was perhaps parliament. He first called his new model parliament in 1295; this was the first time that lords and commoners had been called to work together.

In the 16th century the words 'The Hammer of the Scots' were inscribed on his tomb in Westminster Abbey.

Etal Castle, Northumberland

Etal is a most attractive Northumberland village – its thatched cottages and village inn further enhance the mood of rustic tranquillity. The ruins of Etal Castle can be found at the lower end of the village, overlooking the River Till. The castle really started life as a three-storey tower house, but its position close to the border exposed it to the threat of possible attack by Scottish raiders. It was Sir Robert Manners, knighted on the battlefield by Edward III, who sought and was granted permission to fortify the house in 1342. The improvements, extensions and alterations were carried out by the same masons who built the nearby Ford Castle for Sir William Heron.

Originally it was necessary to cross a drawbridge and go through a narrow passage and a strong gatehouse to enter the building. In fact, the entrance tower is still standing and has an excellent example of a 'murder hole' under one window, which is a hole in the floor of a bay window that allowed defenders to drop missiles, boiling liquids or hot sand – or all three – onto anyone trying to force entry through the doorway below.

In front of the gateway are two ancient cannons from the ill-fated 'Royal George' which sank at Spithead in 1782 with the loss of almost 800 officers and men.

Curtain wall and gatehouse, Etal Castle.

Tower house doorway, Etal Castle.

It is hardly surprising that there was a long-term feud between the Manners family of Etal Castle and the Herons of Ford Castle. This reached a peak in 1427 when Sir John Manners was said to have killed William Heron and one of his companions. The widowed Lady Heron complained to the adjudicating warden's commission that her husband had been killed through malice, but Manners claimed self-defence saying that Heron had attacked his castle with a band of archers and swordsmen. However, the commission decided in favour of Lady Heron, and Manners had to pay her 200 marks compensation and it was ruled that he should also meet the cost of the 500 masses that would be said for the souls of the deceased.

Gatehouse, Etal Castle.

By the beginning of the 1500s the Manners family had moved from Etal and it was left in the care of a constable.

It was one of the castles attacked by King James IV of Scotland on his way to the Battle of Flodden Field. By 1549 it was in the possession of the Crown as part of a project to improve the fortifications of neglected but strategically important border strongholds; however, it was never restored and remains today a romantic ruin on the edge of this idyllic village.

Ferniehirst Castle, Jedburgh

A little over a mile to the south of Jedburgh, a road winds up the side of the valley through the trees to Ferniehirst Castle, traditional home of the Kerrs. The Kerrs have lived in the Borders since the end of the 12th century, and it was Nicol Kerr of Selkirk, one of the Scottish landowners, who put his name to the Ragman Roll paying homage to Edward I in 1296. From the 14th century the Kerrs were more numerous in the area extensive lands and towards the end of the 1300s one of them held the office of Sheriff of Roxburgh.

Andrew Kerr was granted the Jedforest by the Earl of Angus in 1457, and it was his son Thomas who built the original Ferniehirst Castle. Traditionally, in a tower house a turnpike or spiral staircase was built into the thickness of the walls, but, in the case of the Kerrs, because they were all left handed the staircases in their tower houses turned in an anti-clockwise direction to keep their fighting arm free.

About the time of the building of the original Ferniehirst, a dispute over the seniority of the two branches of the family –

Cessford and Ferniehirst – began, and although it occasionally led to a feud it did not prevent inter-marriage between the two. It was not as though they were distant relatives because Sir Thomas Kerr of Ferniehirst was the younger brother of Walter Kerr of Cessford. However, the Cessford line ended with two daughters, one of whom married the head of the Ferniehirst Kerrs.

Perhaps one of the most well-known Kerrs was Robert, who was a particular favourite of King James VI and was knighted by him. He first served as a page and then a gentleman of the bedchamber and accompanied James on his journey south to be crowned James I of England. He was created Earl of Somerset and married Lady Frances Howard, the daughter of the Earl of Suffolk. The Somersets fell out of favour when they were tried for the poisoning of Sir Thomas Overbury. They were sentenced to death but then reprieved and released and finally pardoned within a few years. The evidence against them was by no means conclusive, and some historians believe it may well have been fabricated by personal enemies.

Not long after the Battle of Flodden Field, the castle was taken by the Earl of Surrey after, as he put it, 'long skirmishing and moche difficultie', and Ferniehirst, like many other Scottish castles, fell into English hands.

The garrison made themselves extremely unpopular and greatly feared with the cruelty and bullying they inflicted on the local people. A French officer, serving in Scotland, said of the garrison captain, 'He never came across a young girl but he outraged her, never an old woman that he put her to death with his cruel torture'.

Retribution and punishment came when

Ferniehirst Castle.

the Sieure de Essé and his French troops helped Sir John Kerr to regain his castle. At first the garrison looked like holding out in the tower, but after a long hard struggle the attackers broke through the wall and, realising that the end was probably in sight, the garrison captain came out to try and obtain favourable terms for his men but unconditional surrender was demanded.

News had spread quickly of the attack and soon a bloodthirsty mob gathered at the castle looking for revenge. The captain appeared again to surrender to two French officers, but before they could march him away a Jedburgh man, whose family had suffered outrage and torture at the hands of these English, leapt forward in a blind fury wielding his sword and with one mighty blow struck the Englishman's head from his shoulders. Even as the body fell to the ground the other Scots rushed forward to wash their hands in his blood. They threw the head to each other as if in sport and eventually speared it on a pole and raised it in defiance.

The Scots went on to butcher the garrison – they held a gory competition to see who could cut the most pieces off an English soldier without killing him, and when they ran out of victims they bought further prisoners from the French to continue their bloody torture. One French officer claimed that he swapped a prisoner for a small horse, then the Scots took the man and bound his feet, hands and head together, dropped him in the middle of a field and practised on him with their lances from horseback. When he was dead they cut him into small pieces, which they carried around on the end of their spears in triumph.

In about 1570 Sir Thomas Kerr incurred the displeasure of Queen Elizabeth because of his sympathy with Mary, Queen of Scots. Along with Sir Walter Scott of Buccleuch and the Earl of Westmorland, he led a daring and destructive raid across the border. Queen Elizabeth was furious. She sent an expedition under the Earl of Sussex and Lord Hundson to exact punishment, and Ferniehirst was singled out for special attention.

According to Sussex, 'We could nott blow up Farnhirst – but have so torne ytt with laborars, as ytt were as goode as ley flatt'. However, the old castle was made defendable again, but in 1592 it was destroyed yet again, this time by the army of King James VI, in protest of Sir Andrew Kerr's support for the Earl of Bothwell.

It was rebuilt yet again by Sir Andrew Kerr.

The Fish Garth and Coop House on the River Esk, near Canonbie

The River Esk, or the Border Esk, is recorded as early as 1278 as an outstanding river for salmon such that a law was passed saying that no one was allowed to impede the progress of the salmon upriver to spawn, or the progress of the fry downstream to the sea, by using a net or other means across the river.

Remains of the Fish Garth.

Despite the carefully worded regulations, one of the most bitter and long-lasting disputes between the Scots and the English arose because of an obstruction in the river called the Fish Garth – erected by the English to trap the salmon as they swam upstream. This move upset the Scots who lived near the river above this point to such an extent that they were in a state of constant warfare with the English – bearing in mind of course that the River Esk formed the border line in those days.

The Scots, therefore, claiming they were deprived of a valuable and nutritious food, took the law into their own hands and removed the Fish Garth. In 1474 the question was under heated discussion in London and a commission was set up in 1475 to try and settle the matter. The Bishop of Durham was instructed to meet with the Scots to explain that the English were perfectly entitled to erect a Fish Garth and that such a right had been established by custom for the King of England and his subjects. Needless to say the Scots were in strong disagreement.

By 1485 the garth had been rebuilt but was destroyed again in 1487 by the Scottish Borderers and another commission was set up; by 1488 the members had agreed that each side should appoint three persons as inspectors of the Fish Garth. Even this was unsuccessful, and in 1490 and 1491 the commission met again to discuss this ongoing problem.

Yet another set of commissioners met in 1494 at the 'Lochmabenstone' to try and 'put

Coop House and Fish Garth.

Coop House.

a final end to the controversy as to the Fish Garth' and yet again the English failed to prove their case.

In 1498, however, a certain amount of progress was finally made when it was agreed that any damage done to the Fish Garth should not be regarded as a violation of the peace. And, in the same year, Thomas, Lord Dacre, was granted fishing rights and permission to construct a fish garth, on the Esk by King James IV for a rent of 'four seine of salmond fisch, ilk seine contentand XIIIJ fisch salmond' (at least 100 fish).

However, for a good number of years afterwards the English and the Scots entertained themselves by alternately rebuilding and destroying the garth. Further attempts were regularly made to solve the problem and an uneasy compromise was finally agreed in 1543.

The value placed on the salmon in the Esk was important enough to be included as part of the stakes of single combat which would have been fought between Thomas Howard, the Earl of Surrey, and King James IV before the Battle of Flodden had it not been suggested that King Henry VIII would not meet the agreed terms, no matter what the outcome, and the combat did not take place. They were to have fought for 1) the removal of the Fish Garth and 2) the restoration of Berwick to Scotland.

The nearby Coophouse was, it is thought, in some way connected to the Fish Garth – either as the residence of the person in charge of the fishing or possibly a place where the salmon were taken and stored after being caught.

Ford Castle, Northumberland

Ford Castle stands only six miles from the Scottish border and was built by Odenel de Forde in the late 13th century. His daughter married Sir William Heron, who became the first Lord of the Manor. In 1388 he was granted a licence to fortify the house at Ford, necessary because the Scots, inspired and encouraged by their victory at Bannockburn, were becoming very daring with their incursions into England. They had wasted Northumberland to within four miles of Newcastle and were about to attack the Bishopric of Durham in like manner. However, Sir William was a powerful and tough adversary, well able to take care of himself, and on one occasion when the Scots plundered him of over 600 head of cattle he promptly mounted a counter-foray, lifting 320 cattle, 1,600 sheep, £100 in money, 12/6 in loose change and a pair of socks.

The castle played a prominent role at the time of the Battle of Flodden Field. The then

King James Tower, Ford Castle.

Ford Castle gateway.

owner, another Sir William Heron, was being held prisoner in Fast Castle on the east coast of Scotland and his attractive wife, acutely aware that she was unable to hold out against such a powerful Scottish Army, is said to have approached the Earl of Surrey, asking for his assistance in having Ford spared. Surrey wrote to James offering to release Lord Johnstone and Alexander Home, whom he held as prisoners, if he would spare the castle. James refused, advanced on Ford and made it his headquarters.

It is said that Lady Heron became the king's mistress, and while he dallied the English forces advanced ever nearer. Lady Heron has been accused of betraying James to the English Commander, the Earl of Surrey, but the whole affair seems to have been intricately woven with infatuation, intrigue and passion that has fuelled much

fascinating speculation, but the real truth, perhaps, will never be known. Even James was capable of double dealing – he allowed his troops to pillage and plunder the area while he enjoyed the hospitality offered by Lady Heron.

However ardent the passion between them, it did not stop James from burning the castle and its surrounding village when he moved out to take up his position at Flodden.

Sir William Heron was released after the battle, and after his death in 1536 the castle passed into the ownership of Thomas Carr of Etal and by 1542 had been partially restored, although a considerable part of it was still in ruins – to be eventually rebuilt in the 19th century by Susan, the Marchioness of Waterford, who turned it into the imposing building we see today.

Reiver horses were similar to the small, agile fell pony.

Galloway Nagges or Reiver Horses

The horse or Nagge, as it was referred to, was central to the Reivers' way of life; nagge was merely the name given to a horse for riding, although it has now developed as a derogatory term for an old or infirm animal. These Galloway ponies were ideally suited to the task and the terrain. They had great stamina, were easy to look after, good natured and easily trained. A Galloway had the strength to carry a fully-armed man and yet still displayed the agility to find its way across rough country, almost by instinct, and once

at its destination it had to be mobile and active enough to respond instantly to the commands of its rider when rounding up and driving off herds of cattle or flocks of sheep. The Galloway is admirably portrayed in the Reiver Statue which forms part of the War Memorial in Galashiels. The horse looks out of proportion and too small for the heavily armed man it is carrying – this was the appearance of Reiver and horse and a good description was given by Lord Chief Justice North during a visit to Tynedale in the late 1500s: 'In these perilous times the tenants of each manor were bound to attend on our journey through their respective precincts' – it goes on to describe them as – 'men with long beards, steill helmets, short cloaks, long basket-hilted swords hanging from broad belts and mounted on little horses so that their legs and swords almost touched the ground at every turning'. Sadly, through a series of circumstances, these horses became extinct in the Borders during the 19th century, although good descriptions were recorded by several noted writers. Gervaise Markham, who is credited with introducing the Arab Horse into Britain, wrote of them, in 1600, 'Galloway Nagges are not short of being the best nagges that are bred in any country whatsoever', and Daniel Defoe was quoted in his *Tour Thro' The Whole Island of Great Britain (Letter XII – South West Scotland)* as saying 'They have the best breed of strong, low horses in Britain. These Galloways are remarkable for being good pacers, strong easy goers, hardy, gentle, well broke and above all never tire and are very much bought up in England on that account.'

They stood about 14 hands high with a

Reiver Statue, Galashiels.

shaggy bay or brown coat with black legs and a small head and neck. It is recorded, however, that the Cistercian monks in north-west England were successful in breeding grey animals, preferring that colour to any other. The nearest animal in modern times is perhaps 'The Fell Pony' – itself a rare and protected breed.

Many of the old farmers or, indeed, old countrymen in the north country still refer to horses as 'Gallowers' – another word derived from the riding times in the Borders.

Greenknowe Tower, Gordon

Greenknowe Tower was probably built for James Seton and his wife, Jane Edmonstone, in 1581 – their coats of arms are carved into the lintel above the entrance. The Setons had gained possession of the parish of Gordon through marriage into the Gordon family, who, according to tradition, had been awarded the lands by Malcolm II after the Battle of Careham in 1018.

In the 17th century the tower was purchased by the Pringles of Stichel – it was Walter Pringle of the same family who was a well-known covenanter. However, by 1850 it had been abandoned as a residence and was given into state care by the then owners, the Dalrymple family, who provided a generous donation towards its preservation through their archaeological trust.

Greenknowe is an excellent example of a tower house. There would have been a range of outbuildings built around an enclosed courtyard to the east of the tower and an extensive garden laid out to the west. The approach would have been made through an attractive avenue of trees, while the surrounding land was given over to enclosed farming.

The tower house was in effect a development of the defensive towers of the 13th and 14th centuries and came to be regarded as the traditional style of home suitable for country gentlemen. The thick walls and restricted access provided ample protection from marauders rather than from prolonged siege. The corner turrets had been developed into decorative features and there was no access to a wall walk for defence.

The Lairds Hall would have been situated on the first floor, reached by a spiral staircase from the vaulted basement that would have housed the kitchen and cellar. Above the comfortable living area there would have been access by a further spiral staircase to a series of private rooms and bedrooms and on up to the attic – a much more sophisticated interior than the earlier pele towers.

Tower entrance showing iron 'yett'.

*Previous page:
Greenknowe
Tower.*

The tower was primarily a comfortable home, but in times of trouble it would provide a refuge for the laird and the tenants of his estate and their families. During more settled times it also served as a centre of administration and justice.

Harbottle Castle, Northumberland

Harbottle Castle was once a fortification of great strategic importance. The present castle was originally built by Henry II with support from the Bishopric of Durham on land owned by Odenel de Umfraville. It saw a lot of military action, first over run by William Lion, King of Scots, during his destructive raid into Northumberland, which ended in disaster when he was taken by surprise and captured at Alnwick. William Wallace put the castle under siege in 1296 but gave up after two unsuccessful days, although it did eventually fall to Robert the Bruce in 1318. The castle had been very badly damaged during the Scottish Wars, and in 1336 Gilbert de Umfraville had to seek permission to move his many prisoners to his castle at Prudhoe.

In Tudor times the castle was occupied by Lord Dacre, warden of the English Middle March, who had greatly distinguished himself at the Battle of Flodden, and it was during this time that an event took place at Harbottle that was to change the course of English, and Scottish, history. In 1515 Henry VIII allowed Margaret, his sister, temporary use of the castle during her confinement.

She had been married to James IV of

Harbottle Castle.

Scotland but was widowed when he was killed at Flodden Field. Then a dowager queen, she married Archibald Douglas, Earl of Angus. Within 48 hours of arriving at Harbottle, Margaret gave birth to a daughter – Margaret, Lady Douglas. She was to become Countess of Lennox, mother of Lord Darnley and grandmother of James VI/I. This was only two years after the Battle of Flodden and patriotic feelings were still running high, and as a precaution against any trouble Lord Dacre forbade anyone of Scottish descent from entering Margaret's chamber unless they were under close guard.

The baby was only two days old when Margaret and her party left for Cartington, near Rothbury. Her presence at Harbottle was said to be 'Uneaseful and costly by occasion of the far carriage of everything.'

After the Union of the Crowns in 1603, it was no longer necessary to maintain defence of the area and the castle quickly fell into disrepair. It is said that Harbottle had an iron postern gate almost 7ft high and nearly 4ft wide, plus an iron entrance gate that was over 10ft square. It was possible that these were turned into ploughshares as decreed by James I when he came to the English throne, while the stone walls and towers would provide a ready supply of dressed material for building, particularly by the Widdringtons who used a considerable amount in the construction of their nearby manor house.

Hermitage Castle, Liddesdale

Hermitage Castle stands on the north bank of Hermitage Water at the head of Liddesdale. It is about 12 miles south of Hawick and about six miles north of Newcastleton. Traditionally, it takes its name from a Holy Man who once had a small retreat here. A quarter of a mile to the west of the castle are the remains of a small chapel in a grave yard, and although these ruins date from roughly the same period as the castle they may well stand on the much older site of an earlier building.

Hermitage, or 'the strength of Liddesdale' as it became known, was really the key to the control of a large part of the Border country. It was here that 'The Keeper of Liddesdale'

Hermitage Castle.

Hermitage Chapel.

was based – he enjoyed a unique position distinct from that held by a March warden.

The castle was originally built by the de Soulis family in around 1240, possibly as a wooden motte and bailey construction, and was considered an important Border base. Because of its key location it was much fought over during the Wars of Independence when they broke out in 1296 – it soon fell into English hands but its ownership continued to be hotly disputed by the de Soulis family and their English enemies.

There are many strange, bloody and macabre tales associated with this mysterious, eerie and isolated fortress. Lord

The Cout of Kielder's grave.

William de Soulis has been described as 'A fiend in human form who has committed the blackest of crimes and to whom tradition has ascribed almost every kind and degree of wickedness'.

One tale tells of the unfortunate 'Cout of Kielder', whose grave can be seen to the west of the castle near the chapel. The 'Cout [Colt] of Kielder' was a brave but headstrong young man, much admired for his stature and strength. While he was out hunting with friends on the fells near Hermitage, he chose to ignore the ominous warning that foretold disaster to anyone who should ride widdershins (anti-clockwise) round the mystic Kielder Stone. The cout felt he was well protected from mischief because of his charmed coat of mail and the magic sprigs of holly and rowan on his helmet. His bravado tempted providence and bad luck did befall him and his friends; they were lured into the hands of their deadly enemy, the Lord de Soulis.

At first the party were wined and dined, but it soon became apparent from veiled threats that they were going to be murdered. The young Lord fought his way bravely out of the castle – his companions got to their horses and made good their escape, but de Soulis and his men were hot on the heels of the young cout. De Soulis summoned up the help of the Brown Man of the moors – a malignant demon – who told him that the cout's charms would not protect him in running water. The pursuers chased the young lord towards Hermitage Water, where he stumbled and fell while trying to cross the stream, and they held his head under the water with the point of their lances and the brave young man drowned. The pool where this deed took place is still known as 'The Cout of Kielder's Pool'.

William de Soulis is reputed to have indulged in all kinds of black magic and witchcraft. In 1830 he tried to seize a young lady of the Armstrong family against her wishes, and when riding to her home to do the evil deed he was confronted by her father. A fight broke out and the girl's father was killed. Indeed, de Soulis would have been killed by the crowd who witnessed the murder, but he was saved when the Lord of Mangerton, Alexander Armstrong, dispersed the crowd and escorted de Soulis safely back to Hermitage. The story says that de Soulis was in fact offended because he was rescued by a man he considered to be his social inferior. He then invited Armstrong to a banquet at Hermitage,

supposedly to show his appreciation, but, when Armstrong arrived at the castle, de Soulis violently attacked him, stabbing him to death.

The grieving Armstrongs took Alexander's body to be buried in Ettleton Cemetery. The Minholm Cross was erected by the roadside just below the graveyard in memory of a much loved and highly respected Laird.

There were many vociferous complaints laid with the king about de Soulis and his dreadful behaviour. The king is said to have replied in frustration 'Go boil Lord Soulis and ye list, but let me hear no more of him.' No further excuse was needed as they had a direct order from the king. The local people stormed Hermitage and the story tells that the master magician, Thomas of Ercildoune, fulfilled a prophesy to bind de Soulis in ropes

Nine Stane Rigg.

of sand then, overpowered, he was dragged high up in the hills to the ancient stone circle, Nine Stane Rigg, where:

They rolled him in a sheet of lead
A sheet of lead for a funeral pall;
They plunged him in the cauldron red
And melted him, lead and bones and all.

An excellent tale, but there is evidence to suggest that de Soulis was executed for treason. He was involved in a conspiracy to murder King Robert the Bruce in an attempt to have himself crowned King of Scots. This effectively ended any connections the de Soulis family had with Hermitage.

When Edward Baliol took the throne in 1332 he granted Hermitage to an English knight, Sir Ralph Neville. However, in 1388 Sir William Douglas, 'The Knight of Liddesdale', took Hermitage by force. He was a ruthless man but was much admired for his victories over the English. He was, however, smouldering with fury that David II had not made him Sheriff of Teviotdale, and just to prove his point he imprisoned what he believed to be the wrongly-appointed new Sheriff, Sir Alexander Ramsay, and starved him to death. The king then agreed to Douglas replacing Ramsay in office.

In 1353 Douglas was killed in revenge after he had defected to the English. The next owner of Hermitage was Hugh de Dacre, and he was responsible for rebuilding the castle in stone. The castle then passed to William, the 1st Earl of Douglas, who transformed Dacre's castle into a huge, solid tower. William died in 1384 and his son James was killed at the Battle of Otterburn in 1388. Hermitage then came into the possession of George, the 1st Earl of Angus and founder of the 'Red Douglases'.

Initially, the Red Douglases were loyal supporters of the Crown, even when their kinsmen, 'The Black Douglases', rose against James II. It was, however, Archibald 'Bell the Cat', the 5th Earl and warden of the Middle March, who cautiously sided with the English, and although he did help put James IV on the throne in 1488 he was still distrusted. By 1492 he had worked out a plan that in the event of a war he would receive beneficial treatment from the English if he made sure that Hermitage did not fall into the hands of another Scottish Lord. The plan was discovered and the king decided that Archibald was not to be trusted with such an important Scottish castle, and he was forced to exchange Hermitage for Bothwell Castle in Lanarkshire.

Patrick Hepburn, Earl of Bothwell, was the next owner of Hermitage. By the time the castle had passed to the 3rd Earl, his loyalty was also called into question, and he spent several years in prison and exile and into the bargain was forced to hand over the ownership of Hermitage to James V. He did no better after James's death and served another term in prison after the accession of the infant Mary, Queen of Scots for trying to hand over Hermitage to the English.

James Hepburn, the 4th Earl of Bothwell, also enjoyed a less than savoury reputation – he was implicated in the murder of Henry, Lord Darnley, Mary, Queen of Scots' second husband, only to marry her shortly afterwards, and that did not last because he left her that same summer to flee into exile and never return.

It was, however, while he was Keeper of

Liddesdale that he was injured in a fight by Little Jock Elliot of the Park, a well known Reiver, and was rushed back to Hermitage to recover from his wounds. Mary, Queen of Scots was on her annual tour and just happened to be in Jedburgh when she heard about the incident. The couple were already romantically linked, but she confirmed the rumours by riding the 25 miles in bad weather to visit Bothwell. She was only with him for two hours because she was still married to Lord Darnley and dare not stay at the castle. She had to make the return ride to Jedburgh in inclement weather, and unfortunately during the journey her horse fell into a bog and she contracted a fever which was very nearly fatal.

Francis Stewart, Bothwell's nephew, was the next owner of the castle. He was a well educated but unstable and violent man. He was constantly in conflict with James VI, but this did him no good because he was eventually sent into permanent exile.

Sir Walter Scott of Buccleuch, or 'The Bold Buccleuch' as he became known, was the next Keeper Of Liddesdale. He gained a degree of notoriety for his part in the rescue of Kinmont Willie Armstrong from Carlisle Castle in 1569, but in a few years the days of the Border Reivers were numbered. In 1603 James VI travelled to London to become James I of England and almost immediately he began his 'Pacification of the Borders'. Buccleuch enthusiastically gave his help to this without a shred of remorse or guilt, and this eventually brought about the end of Hermitage as a mighty strategic fortress. However, its romantic history lived on and even Sir Walter Scott had his portrait painted with Hermitage as the backdrop.

Home Castle, Roxburghshire

The original lands of Hume were granted to William of Hume sometime before 1214, and it is from this original seat that the family

Home Castle.

takes its name. The Humes, or Homes, are one of the most prominent names in the history Scotland and the Borders. They achieved the great distinction of being the only frontier family who could claim continuous domination in their own March and usually held the position of wardens of the Scottish East March. Although they often incurred the displeasure of the Scottish Crown and got themselves into serious trouble, they still managed to hold on to their eminence and influence.

Home Castle is an excellent example of an early Scottish castle built round a rectangular courtyard plan. Because of the extensive views it commands, it was used as a signal station and a beacon could be lit here to warn of invasion by the English. This was the only castle in the Borders not destroyed by Robert the Bruce's extreme scorched earth policy in 1313.

In 1460 King James II and his Queen, Mary of Gueldres, stayed here during the siege of Roxburgh Castle when it was held by the English; King James was killed by an exploding gun during this action.

The Duke of Somerset captured Home Castle in 1547 in spite of its defences having been recently strengthened by the French, and after stiff resistance by Lady Home, whose husband had recently been killed at the Battle of Pinkie. The English spent £700 on repairs, only to have it taken from them the following year by the Homes, who then used it as a storage place for captured English guns.

However, in 1569 the Earl of Sussex recaptured the castle with a force of over 1,000 horses and five great cannon.

It was reduced to a ruin by artillery

Housesteads Bastle.

bombardment when it was attacked by Oliver Cromwell in 1651, but it was bought and rebuilt in its present form by the Third Lord Marchmont, one of the Home family, in the late 1700s.

Housesteads Bastle House

Housesteads is possibly the best preserved fort on Hadrian's Wall, but the Border Reivers have also left their mark on this site of great interest to roman historians.

The south gateway of the fort was converted to a bastle – a small, two-storey fortified farm house – in the 17th century. It provided a home for one Hugh Nixon, a cattle thief and reputed receiver of stolen goods, and also a close associate of the infamous Armstrong family.

The bastle was built against the south wall of the fort just to the east of the original south gateway, using the readily-available supply of dressed Roman stone to create the four-feet thick walls. Extra accommodation was added, together with a small corn-drying mill. There are also the remains of an outer staircase – a feature typical of bastle houses of the 17th century.

In 1600 the area was visited by the noted historian and cartographer William Camden, and he observed that he could not safely

Housesteads Bastle.

undertake a full survey of the area because of the dangerous robbers hereabouts. Although they presented a danger to travellers, the Reivers probably inadvertently helped to preserve Housesteads by also keeping other people away who wished to plunder the site for building materials.

Jedburgh Abbey

Jedburgh Abbey is an impressive sight, situated on the terraced banks of the River Jed at the edge of the town. What was to become Jedburgh Abbey was founded by David I before he was King of Scots. He started his programme of monastic foundations in 1113, and in 1118 he invited a group of Augustinian Canons from St Quentin in France to establish a priory at Jedburgh. David granted lands and fisheries to this priory and it prospered so quickly it was made an abbey in 1154. Its importance rapidly increased during the second half of the 12th century and continued well into the 13th century. King Malcolm 'The Maiden' died here in 1195.

Reputedly it was here, at the wedding of Alexander III to Yolande de Dreux, that a ghost appeared to warn of the king's death – in 1286 he fell over a cliff from his horse, at Kinghorn in Fife, on his way to visit his queen.

Jedburgh Abbey was also in an important strategic position. It was on the main Carlisle to Edinburgh road and lay only 10 miles from the border with Northumberland. However, this made it vulnerable to attack during the wars with England. Repeated attacks, destruction and raids in the 15th and 16th centuries meant it was necessary to do a lot of building and repairs, and by 1545 the Abbey was governed by Commandators of the Home family. The abbey was finally destroyed by the army of Henry VIII in the second half of the 16th century.

Scotland's best scholars and intellectuals

Jedburgh Abbey.

Deputy Captain of Norham Castle. However, in 1527 he got into serious trouble with Roger Heron, the then Sheriff of Northumberland. Lisle was found guilty of disobeying the orders of Cardinal Wolsey, and he also threw in a few insults for good measure. Through this behaviour and several other misdeeds he found himself imprisoned in Newcastle.

Also imprisoned in the notorious Black Gate at that time were 'divers theeves of Scotland and traytors of Tynedale', which included in their number a notable catch in the person of John (Jock) Armstrong of the Side – a tower in Liddesdale that stood almost at the confluence of Hermitage and Liddel Waters – who had been captured during a raid into Northumberland. Jock o' the Side was well known for his exploits, and he was also a nephew of Mangerton, heidman of the Armstrongs, who swore to

came from the areas around the Border abbeys. The most well known was, perhaps, John Duns Scotus from Duns in Berwickshire. He was known as 'the subtle doctor' – a renowned free thinker, he established the foundations of the Scottish theory and tradition of philosophy.

Jock o' the Side's escape from Newcastle

One of the most famous escapes in Border history was that of Jock o' the Side from Newcastle. The story really begins with the Lisle family, who had once been Lords of Redesdale. Sir William Lisle was the roguish and unpredictable head of the family, and his dangerous and daring exploits against the Scots had once earned him the position of

Black Gate, Newcastle.

Newcastle city walls.

rescue him and got together a group of men from Liddesdale to carry out this promise.

There was Mangerton, the Laird's Jock and the Laird's Wat – both his sons – and it has been suggested that among the other two or three riders was the notorious Hobbie Noble of Bewcastle.

Time was of the utmost importance because young Jock may well have been hung without trial, so the little expedition disguised themselves as 'Cadgers' – itinerant merchants – and crossed the River Tyne near Chollerford, stopping only to make themselves a ladder from a tree they had cut down. They arrived in Newcastle to find their ladder – as often happens in these escapades – too short. Not to be defeated, they broke out Lisle and his son and with their help rescued young Jock, even though he was manacled hand and foot with 'a full 15 stane o' Spanish iron'. He was therefore forced to ride side saddle during the escape 'like only

bride', and to create further difficulty when they arrived back at the Tyne they found the river in flood. Young Wat – 'the Laird's saft Wat, the greatest coward in the companie' argued against trying to cross a river in spate with a man weighed down by so much iron – but after much heated discussion they crossed the river and made it safely back to Liddesdale, along with the Lisles, who, having nowhere else to go, became full members of the Armstrong riders who operated out of Liddesdale and turned to a life of raiding, and eventually had the wardens of both countries baying for their blood.

Johnnie Armstrong of Gilnockie

A memorial stone in Carlenrig Cemetery, just off the road between Langholm and Hawick, records the fate of Johnnie Armstrong of Gilnockie, one of the more well known, and perhaps the most romanticised, of that notorious Border family.

'TRADITION RECORDS

THAT NEAR THIS SPOT WERE BURIED

JOHNNIE ARMSTRONG OF GILNOCKIE

AND

A NUMBER OF HIS PERSONAL FOLLOWERS

WHO WERE TREACHEROUSLY TAKEN AND EXECUTED

AT CARLANRIGG BY ORDER OF KING JAMES V

DURING HIS EXPEDITION TO PACIFY THE BORDERS

IN JULY 1530

"JOHN MURDRED WAS AT CARLINRIGG

AND ALL HIS GALLANT COMPANIE

BUT SCOTLAND'S HEART WAS NE'ER SAE WAE

TO SEE SAE MONY BRAVE MEN DIE"

OLD BALLAD

THIS STONE ERECTED SEPTEMBER 1897'

Johnnie was Sim the Laird's brother and a relative of Kinmont Willie, and his tower, Gilnockie, overlooked the River Esk near Cannonbie. Although legend has it that his home was Hollows Tower, some historians believe it was originally built high above the river at the eastern edge of Gilnockie Bridge and possibly some of the stone from this now demolished tower actually provided material for the construction of the bridge.

The circumstances that shaped the story of Johnnie of Gilnockie really started in the early part of the 16th century. Although England and Scotland were technically at peace at that time, King Henry VIII was actively encouraging the English and the Scots to feud, and also encouraging his own wardens to mount reprisal raids in return for any incursions by the Scots, and by 1529 the Borders were in turmoil – the usual inevitable cycle of constant raid and reprisal.

In 1530 James V was keen to calm the situation and to establish a lasting peace. Although he was only 17 years old, James met the situation with a hard line – he arrested the Earl of Bothwell, the Lords Home and Maxwell and the Lairds of Buccleuch, Ferniehirst, Polwarth and Johnstone and imprisoned them all in Edinburgh. Others were not so fortunate. Adam Scott of Tushielaw, or the 'King of Thieves', as he was known, was accused of a series of serious crimes ranging from robbery, suppressing and oppressing his tenants to 'theftuously taking blackmail'.

William Cockburn of Henderland was also arrested; his crimes were high treason, robbery and harbouring dangerous criminals.

Tradition has it that Cockburn and Scott were forcibly pulled out of their own front doors and strung up – Cockburn over his own gate and Scott on the nearest tree. However, there are contradicting records that they were both taken to Edinburgh, tried and beheaded – 'Their heidis fixit upon the Tolbuith of Edinburg.'

Even though her husband was executed in Edinburgh, one of the most moving of all the Border Ballads is attributed to Marjorie Cockburn, 'The Border Widow's Lament':

There came a man by middle day
He spied his sport and went away:
And brought the king that very night
Who broke my bower and slew my knight.

He slew my knight to me sae dear;
He slew my knight and poin'd (stole) his gear;
My servants all for life did flee
And left me in extremitie…

Having dealt with these miscreants, James turned his full attention to the redoubtable Johnnie Armstrong of Gilnockie. The story has it that the king sent Gilnockie a 'loving letter, written in his own fair hand' inviting him to meet his 'liege lord' at Carlenrig, about nine miles south of Hawick.

The fact that Armstrong neither obtained, nor indeed sought, safe conduct goes to prove that he thought he and his men were in no apparent danger. In fact, the day of the meeting Johnnie Armstrong is said to have had a rousing assembly with his followers and that they all took part in friendly sport before they dressed in their finest clothes and, in the Reiver tradition, rode out fully armed to meet the king. Johnnie arrived at Carlenrig with about 50 riders, and no doubt they expected to be offered pardons for their raiding and robbery – after all Armstrong was very proud of the fact that he had never 'spoyled' a Scot and all his activities had been directed exclusively at the English. It is quite possible that James meant no harm to Gilnockie and his men, but, when he was faced with their superior brash self confidence and saw how ostentatiously dressed they were and, of course, so heavily armed, he ordered his guards to close in on them. According to some historians, this was the moment James made up his mind to deal with the robber and his gang. The king is believed to have asked 'What wants yon knave that a king should have?' He then turned and told his guards to 'take this tyrant out of my sight!' They were to be taken and hanged. Armstrong began to plead for his life, but possibly his attitude in his response was wrong – it certainly did not help his position – as he offered boastfully to bring the king any English subject, of any rank, at any time of day. He even offered to share the income from his blackmail racket with the king, but James would have nothing to do with Johnnie Armstrong – after all, Scotland was not technically at war with England and yet Armstrong was raiding and causing havoc with this supposedly friendly neighbour – there could be only one punishment. As he was led to the gallows, Armstrong's final proud words to the king were 'I am but a fool to seek

Hollows Tower.

Opposite: Kelso Abbey.

grace at a graceless face.' He also lamented that King Henry would give his horses weight in gold to see him hanged. This was true: the records state that the people of England were 'exceedingly glad that Johnnie Armstrong was executed.'

Gilnockie and most of his followers were hanged at Carlenrig – although about a dozen of the men were taken to Edinburgh for execution. King James thought that this action would ease the volatile situation in the Borders, but in fact he lost the last shreds of loyalty to the Crown because many of the Armstrongs moved to Cumberland and renewed their reiving with a determined vigour, fired by the treachery that their kinsmen had suffered at the hands of their monarch.

Kelso Abbey

Kelso is possibly in one of the most attractive locations of all Border towns. It sits comfortably in the centre of the wide valley of the Lower Tweed. It was the nearby castle and town of Roxburgh that were originally the more important, but Kelso gradually expanded in the shadow of the abbey. By the 15th century the importance of Roxburgh had declined because of the Border wars and many of the inhabitants had moved out to settle on the other side of the river in Kelso.

The abbey originally belonged to a reformed Benedictine or Tironensian order of monks, who came to Selkirk from France at the invitation of David in 1113 before he took the throne. After he was crowned in 1128, he established Roxburgh as a Royal Burgh, and the monks were moved from Selkirk to Kelso on the advice of the Bishop of Glasgow. The abbey took about 75 years to build and became the largest and the second most wealthy of Scotland's religious houses. It was an important religious centre. In 1152 the king's son, Henry, Earl of

Kelso Abbey.

Northumberland, was buried in the abbey and both James III and James IV were crowned there.

Kelso Abbey, like Dryburgh, Jedburgh and Melrose, suffered severe raids by the English Army during the Wars of Independence in the early 1300s – it was attacked by Edward II and repaired and partly rebuilt by Richard I. It was finally destroyed in 1544 when Sir Ralph Eure, warden of the March, turned his attention on Kelso after attacking Jedburgh. Among his army were a large number of Scottish Nixons and Crosers from Liddesdale, along with Olivers and Rutherfords from Teviotdale, who had all sworn allegiance to Henry VIII. During that final devastating attack on Kelso Abbey, a handful of local men, together with a few monks, held the abbey tower with fierce determination right to the bitter end.

After this monumental raid, the Scots, with help from the English, added insult to injury by raiding their own border, systematically destroying everything they came across.

Kinmont Willie

Kinmont Willie is possibly one of the most well-known Border Reivers because of his rescue from Carlisle Castle by 'the Bold Buccleuch'. This notable event is commemorated in one of the most famous of the Border Ballads.

Will Armstrong of Kinmont was born in about 1530 in the Scottish West March, and his tower was at Woodhouselee on the River Esk. He was married to Hutchen Graham's daughter, his sister was married to another of the Grahams and his daughter married the notorious Thomas Carleton of Gilsland. He was also closely involved with the Maxwells, one of whom, at that time, held the office of March warden, and he actively encouraged Kinmont's forays into England. His band of Reivers were known as 'Kinmont's Bairns', and they rode out from the safety of the Debateable Land to mount raids into Northumberland and Cumberland at will. Their savage action did not stop with the English Marches because they often plundered their own side of the border into the bargain, but Kinmont was protected by the powerful Maxwells and, indeed, seemed to live a charmed existence.

Kinmont Willie had made a bitter enemy of Thomas, Lord Scrope, warden of the English West March, against whose area most of his raids had been directed. There is record of such a raid being mounted with over 1,000 horsemen from Liddesdale, Annandale and Ewesdale, who lifted over 3,000 head of sheep, goats and cattle. His persistent raiding and disregard for Scrope's authority led to a desperate approach being made to the Scottish king by the English warden to ask that someone be appointed to keep Kinmont Willie and his men under control. The king replied that he would seek an assurance of good behaviour from Kinmont. Scrope's approach to the king only served to upset Sir

Postern Gate, Carlisle Castle.

Walter Scott of Buccleuch, who had been recently appointed Keeper of Liddesdale, where many of the Armstrongs lived. He took Scrope's action as a personal insult; not only had he been by-passed in the approach to the king, but doubt had also been cast on his integrity and his ability to do his job. Buccleuch and Scrope were both young and ambitious, and a confrontation of some sort was inevitable. It came to a head in the middle of March 1596.

A Day of Truce, held at Kershopefoot, was attended by the two deputy wardens, Scott for the Scottish West March and Salkeld for the English. The day was also attended by Kinmont Willie who, in line with the privileges afforded by a Day of Truce, felt secure in the knowledge that he could not be arrested.

When the meeting was drawn to a close, everyone made their way home. Kinmont rode part of the way with Robert Scott, the Scottish Deputy, and once they parted he continued with a few of his associates towards his tower at Woodhouselee. Also going home, on the other side of the river, was the English deputy warden Salkeld with about 200 of his men. Just before the confluence of the Liddel and the Esk at Rowanburnfoot, the English took the opportunity to hastily ford the river, and after a short struggle they captured Kinmont Willie. He was tied to his horse with his arms behind him and taken to Carlisle – according to the Scots.

The Musgraves, who had been with Salkeld, ventured that they had come upon Kinmont Willie by accident when they raided a house in Harelaw to capture a party of outlaws. He had tried to rally men against them and so they arrested him for their own safety and delivered him to Salkeld.

It would seem, however, that the Scots were probably right, according to the evidence of the events that unfolded afterwards. The arrest of Kinmont Willie, in what was deemed to be a flagrant disregard of the only injunction to which they would pay any heed, caused an outrage on both sides of the border, particularly with Walter Scott of Buccleuch in whose area of authority it had happened.

Still boiling with fury from what he considered to be a personal insult, Buccleuch wrote to Scrope demanding the immediate release of Kinmont Willie; his demands were dismissed out of hand. Buccleuch even tried to approach the English ambassador at the Scottish court, but to no avail. The English wardens had suffered years of raiding by Kinmont and his 'bairns,' and Scrope was not about to give up the opportunity to end the problem once and for all.

Buccleuch decided to take matters into his own hands and mount a rescue attempt. Carlisle Castle was probably the most secure building in the Borders, and any raid would be a difficult and extremely dangerous task. Buccleuch recruited some of the finest riders

in the Borders to undertake the mission, and the final plans were made at Langholm race meeting.

With everything agreed, the party assembled at Morton, one of Kinmont's Towers in the Debateable Land, about 10 miles from Carlisle, on the evening of 13 April 1596.

The Bold Buccleuch set off for Carlisle in the pouring rain with about 100 hardened Border Reivers. Naturally, the Armstrongs were heavily involved, but there were also a large number of Scotts, Elliots and Grahams who took part, including Auld Wat of Harden, John Elliot of Copshaw, Christie of Barngleish, John of Hollows and the Laird of Mangerton, chief of the Armstrongs.

Scouts rode ahead, followed by an assault party equipped with ladders, crowbars, ropes and assorted tools to break into the castle. Buccleuch and the main party followed behind. They crossed the flooded River Eden and arrived at the castle two hours before

Tower of Sark churchyard, said to be the last resting place of Kinmont Willie.

dawn. Luckily the bad weather had driven the castle watch to seek cover and the Reivers approached the walls unseen. Unfortunately their scaling ladders were found to be too short, but a quick search revealed a small oak postern gate in the west wall of the castle. Using the continuing bad weather to their advantage, Buccleuch's men undermined the door, allowing it to be opened. Several men were left at the gate to cover the retreat, while Buccleuch and about 25 of his men swiftly made their way to the part of the castle his spies had told him that Kinmont was being held. The alarm was raised, but it was too late. Buccleuch and his party, together with a grateful Kinmont, quickly made for the river – once across they galloped back into the darkness from whence they had come…

The torrential fury of white water that was the Eden prevented any pursuit, and Scrope was left to account for the loss of his infamous prisoner.

He was fairly sure that the rescue had been partly an 'inside job', and that several of the Grahams were involved. He extended his enquiries and discovered that Thomas Carleton and Richie Graham of Brackenhill had also been part of the operation. The rescue created a political uproar between the two countries, and Scrope continued to try to gain some recompense by mounting ever-increasing warden's raids into Scotland. On one occasion a complaint was laid against him when he personally led an army of 2,000 men into Liddesdale, devastated over four square miles, tied his prisoners together like dogs and left about 70 young children stripped of their clothes, and it was said that 10 of them died of cold eight days later. The English were unmoved and pointed out that the raid had taken place at the height of summer.

Undeterred by his unfortunate experience, Kinmont Willie continued to ride, this time with 'Sandies Bairns'. He was also taking part in the forbidden practice of buying English horses to sell in Scotland, and, of course, he suffered another raid on his home, a reprisal for horse stealing. Scrope continued to 'exact revenge' against Kinmont Willie because of the great embarrassment his escape caused. It was carried out to such an extent that eventually King James lodged a complaint against his behaviour.

Eventually Kinmont Willie died, but his name is remembered in ballad and fable and as a reminder of a Day Of Truce wrongly violated.

Tradition has it that Kinmont Willie is laid to rest in the Tower of Sark graveyard in the Debateable Land.

Kirkhope Tower, Ettrickbridge

Kirkhope Tower is located in the Ettrick Valley, about half a mile to the north west of the village of Ettrickbridge and about six miles west of Selkirk. It was built in the 1500s by Walter Scott of Harden, or 'Auld Wat' as he was known. He was probably one of the most infamous Border Reivers of his day. It was he who was fortunate enough to marry 'The Flower of Yarrow' – the beautiful Marion Scott of Dryhope. Auld Wat has always been portrayed as a larger than life, humorous character, although the records of the day do confirm that he did his fair share of robbery, looting and killing. There is one particular incident on record when he and his associates rode with the Elliots on Gilsland with over

*Previous page:
Kirkhope Tower.*

400 men and burned 20 houses, stole over £400 worth of goods and made off with over 300 head of livestock, and wounded several of the victims just to add injury to insult. He was regarded as an important man in the Borders and was invited to take part in the ill-fated raid by the Earl of Bothwell when he attempted to take James VI prisoner; however, Auld Wat had his tower at Harden destroyed for his part in the operation.

Another story tells of how, when one of his sons was killed by a rival group of Scotts, he stopped his family from taking revenge by locking them up while he himself travelled to Edinburgh to secure a grant of the murderers lands by way of compensation, explaining to the rest of the family that it was worth losing one of his family for what he had gained.

Auld Wat was one of the party who carried out the daring rescue of Kinmont Willie Armstrong from Carlisle Castle.

His most famous comment, perhaps, was made as he passed a haystack on the way back from a raid; he looked at it sideways and was heard to say 'Aye, if ye had fower legs ye wouldna stand there lang'. And, of course, he was one of Sir Walter Scott's ancestors, and it was probably his memory that fired Sir Walter's undying love and interest in the history of the Borders.

*Lanercost Bridge
once carried the
main Carlisle to
Newcastle turnpike.*

Lanercost Priory, Brampton

King Henry II captured the area of Gilsland from the Scots in 1157 and appointed Hubert de Vaux as Lord of the Manor. The king encouraged the foundation of a new monastery in the area, and it is traditionally accepted that Robert de Vaux, son of Hubert de Vaux, established the Augustinian Priory at Lanercost in 1164, in memory of his father.

The priory is sited in a tranquil, secluded, wooded spot in the attractive valley of the River Irthing, alongside the site of the ancient route from Newcastle to Carlisle. Regardless of their idyllic position, religious houses still made attractive targets for marauding armies and Lanercost did not escape attention. In the years after the Battle of Bannockburn, raids were frequent and the monastery suffered several attacks during these years, although two were particularly savage – by the Earl of Buchan in 1296 and by William Wallace in 1297 on his rampage through the North of England.

Lanercost bears the distinction that it is the only English Monastery that has been a royal residence – this was for almost six months when Edward I visited in 1306. He was on yet another military campaign against the Scots in spite of his age and poor health. He was so ill that he had to be carried on a litter – consequently, his group made extremely slow progress on their journey to Carlisle, and Lanercost was where they called a halt. The king was accompanied by Queen Margaret plus their numerous supporters and servants, probably over 200 people in all, and they all had to be accommodated at the priory.

Lanercost Priory.

The king had arrived at the end of September but was too ill to continue his journey until the following March, putting a severe strain on the finances of the monastery. The monks bitterly complained that they had been 'greatly impoverished' by his sojourn – there is a record that over 200 deer were killed during the stay of the Royal party. King Edward did not let his illness interfere with his dedicated persecution of the Scots because, while he was at Lanercost, the two captured brothers of Robert the Bruce were brought before him. He sent Thomas to Carlisle, where he was to be dragged around the city by horses and then executed and his head displayed on a spike on the city gates, and Alexander was to have his head cut off immediately and also displayed on a spike on the city gates.

After the death of Edward I, the Scots resumed their large-scale raids with enthusiasm, and in 1311 Robert the Bruce invaded the priory for three days. Although there was only a small amount of structural impairment, sacred vessels were damaged, treasure chests looted and religious artefacts wantonly destroyed. The unfortunate priors

Lanercost Priory.

suffered this awful depredation while they were still recovering from the visit from Edward I.

The monks suffered another serious blow in 1346 when King David II and his army plundered the priory on his way to a resounding defeat at the Battle of Nevilles Cross near Durham. These raids on top of a widespread famine and rampant cattle disease in 1316, followed by the outbreak of the Black Death in 1349, must have caused the community serious difficulties. And in 1386 the prior of Lanercost was captured by Scottish raiders and ransomed.

However, over the next century things gradually improved and the priory did recover, until the Dissolution of the Monasteries in 1536. On 4 March 1537 Henry VIII sent the Duke of Norfolk to close the priory, and although he did offer a temporary reprieve it was finally closed in January 1538.

The priory eventually came into the possession of Thomas Dacre, who fought at the Battle of Solway Moss and distinguished himself in the rank of deputy warden of the English West March in 1552. He converted part of the monastery to a private residence and created a garden, an orchard, a rabbit warren and built a dovecote in the grounds.

Lanercost eventually passed to the Howard family, in January 1929 it was passed over into State Guardianship and today it is in the care of English Heritage.

Langholm Castle

The Black Douglasses were heavily defeated in the Battle of Arkinholme in 1455, and shortly after this the Maxwells emerged as the dominant family.

It was Robert, Lord Maxwell, who granted Johnnie Armstrong, under the Bond of Manrent, the lands at Langholm and Upper Eskdale in 1525, but it was

Langholm Castle.

Christopher Armstrong of Banglies, Johnnie's brother, who built Langholm Castle in 1528 – it measured 50ft by 30ft with walls almost 6ft thick and would probably have been a fortified tower rather than a castle. In 1530 Johnnie Armstrong and his brother were hanged at Teviothead by King James V and the castle passed into royal possession. However, it was retaken and 'spoyled' by the Armstrongs of Liddesdale in 1544 and continued to change hands up until the end of the 1500s. Indeed, it saw a deal of intrigue when the plan for the rescue of Kinmont Willie was discussed here in 1596. After the Union of the Crowns in 1603, King James sent 1,000 mounted soldiers and over 200 leveys with orders to destroy all the fortified buildings in Liddesdale, including Langholm Castle.

The Clan Armstrong Museum is sited near the ruins of Langholm Castle and provides a comprehensive and fascinating history of that most notorious of the Riding families and their associates. Today the castle is in the care of the Buccleuch Estates.

Liddel Castle, near Newcastleton

The site of Liddel Castle can be found on the B6357 to the north of Newcastleton, just past the cemetery. The original castle is thought to have been built by the earliest Lord of Liddesdale during the 11th century, and it was probably one of the first in the Borders to be built in stone by the Normans.

Unsettlingly, in 1207 a later Lord de Soulis was killed in the castle by his servants. In 1207 Henry III ordered the Sheriff of Cumberland to take possession of the castle to defend it against the Scots, and it was here in 1296 that Edward I stayed overnight when he made the journey from Roxburgh Castle to Liddesdale.

Liddel Castle.

Lochmaben Castle.

By 1319 it was in the possession of John de Mareschal and John de Prendregest, who had deserted the English to join the Scots. In 1328 it passed to the Wakes of Liddell by the generosity of Edward III. However, in 1346 it fell to the Scottish King David II who, before going on to fight the Battle of Nevilles Cross in Durham, destroyed the castle of 'Lidallis on the Marches'.

By the 18th century the castle and the surrounding village of Castleton had become a ruin, and the Duke of Buccleuch allocated a site a couple of miles down the road on which Newcastleton was built.

Lochmaben Castle

Lochmaben lies between the towns of Dumfries and Lockerbie and its castle is sited in a strong defensive position on a promontory projecting north from the southern shore of Castle Loch. This is the second castle in the area – the first was built in the mid-12th century by the Bruce family and some historians believe that this was actually the birthplace of Robert the Bruce. The first building was probably constructed

from wood, although it is thought that it was eventually rebuilt in stone. It was captured by Edward I in 1298, and it was he who ordered the building of a new fortress, making better use of the naturally defendable terrain. By 1299 work on the new building must have been advanced enough to withstand an attack from Robert the Bruce, although it was not finally completed until the early 1300s.

The design was quite unusual. It was effectively sited on two islands separated by a moat, or canal, connected to the loch at both ends but protected by side walls carried on arches over the canal. This would ensure a sheltered and protected harbour for boats to unload unhindered. The inner ward, built of stone, was the most northerly and well protected of the two sections, while the outer ward, to the south, probably had wooden

Lochmaben Castle.

defences and provided a home for most of the inhabitants of the castle.

Lochmaben changed hands between the English and the Scots several times during the 1300s. It was captured by Robert the Bruce in 1306 and quickly retaken by the English but then surrendered back to the Scots in 1314 after the Battle of Bannockburn. The English were back in 1333 until the charismatic Archibald the Grim, 3rd Earl of Douglas and Lord of Galloway, took possession for the Scots once again in 1384.

James II took control of Lochmaben when he destroyed the Black Douglases in the Battle of Arkinholme in 1455, and James V gathered his army here in 1542 before going on to disastrous defeat at the hands of the English at the Battle of Solway Moss.

Mary, Queen of Scots attended a banquet here with Lord Darnley in September 1565 before returning to Edinburgh. They had been all over southern Scotland with an army in pursuit of her half brother the Earl of Moray after he had taken up arms against her in protest over her wedding to Darnley, earlier the same year. Moray eventually fled to Carlisle.

The last action at Lochmaben was in 1588 when James VI mounted a successful siege to recapture it from the rebellious Maxwell family.

After the Union of the Crowns there was no further need for a castle to serve as a stronghold in the wars between England and Scotland, and the castle gradually fell into disuse and was subsequently systematically stripped of its dressed stone, leaving the stark ruins we see today, which serve as a grim reminder of the dark days of the Border wars.

Low Cleughs Bastle, near West Woodburn, Northumberland

The hillside ruin of Low Cleughs Bastle can be found about a mile west of West

Woodburn along the Bellingham Road. It is thought to have been built just before 1600. Farmers, who were a little better off than the average person, would be able to build these dwellings. The walls are over 3ft thick and the small windows place the emphasis firmly on defence. Bastles usually consisted of a lower basement, for sheltering livestock, which supported an upper floor where the farmer and his family would live.

Low Cleughs is unusual in that the upper doorway is sited directly above the lower doorway, about a third of the way along the south side. This upper doorway must have been added a little later when the need for ease of access was greater than the necessity of defence, because in the earlier times access to the upper floor would have been by ladder through an aperture which could have been easily blocked in times of danger.

Mangerton Tower.

Low Cleughs was abandoned in the mid-1800s but stands today as a fine example of a fortified Northumbrian farm house.

Mangerton Tower, Liddesdale

Mangerton Tower stands beside the trackbed of the old Waverley Railway line on the eastern bank of Liddel Water, about a mile to the south of Newcastleton. Only a small part of what has obviously been a substantial tower remains – there seems to be an informed opinion that it was possibly the building of the railway that caused some of the destruction. Sir Walter Scott seemed to think that these were the remains of a water mill which was built of stones from the old tower, but necessarily a mill would have to be beside the river and there is no trace of the watercourse being changed. Furthermore a well-weathered stone tablet built into the wall bears the coat of arms of the Armstrongs, the date of 1583 and two sets of initials – SA and EE – those of Sim Armstrong and his wife Elizabeth Elliot.

Traditionally, the Lairds of Mangerton were always the head of the Armstrong Clan – these charismatic men were among the most notable Reivers of their time. Archie Armstrong is mentioned in the Border Papers of 1547 at the time when there was a sudden increase in reiving activity in the West March. Sir George Wharton, the warden, felt it was necessary to mount an expedition, under the leadership of Sir Thomas Carleton, to restore some sort of order. Raiding by the Johnstones and Maxwells into Cumbria had reached an unacceptable level, and in order to put a stop to this Wharton invited some Scots to help him – he mentions 'The Old Laird of

Mangerton Tower.

Mangerton and his son and others of Liddesdale as being willing to serve his purpose'. It was young Archie of Mangerton who took part in a cunning two-ambush plan that led to the capture of the Laird of Johnstone. Wharton lured Johnstone out of his tower by sending some men to burn his brother's home. The laird left his own tower at Lochwood to avenge the attack and rode straight into an ambush by the Captain of Langholm and his men. Johnstone, however, was ready for this and, striking hard, he captured some of the ambushers and set off in pursuit of the remainder. However, a second ambush was waiting – 300 men led by the warden's son, John Musgrave, and Archie Armstrong. The Johnstones fought bravely but over 100 were taken prisoner and many others were killed or wounded. Johnstone himself put up a good fight, but in the end he was captured. This opened up the opportunity for the Armstrongs and their associates to capture the Johnstone's Tower at Lochwood.

Riding with the English had been profitable. However, the Armstrongs of Mangerton did not always have things their own way and even they had to complain to the March warden occasionally, as several entries for Martinmas 1587 confirm.

'The Laird of Mangerton complains upon Cuddie Taylor, John Taylor and their complices; at two times for taking 200 kie and oxen, insight £20.00 sterling.'

And…

'The Laird of Mangerton complains upon Adam's Jamie Foster, Matthew Taylor, Skailbe's Hutchin and Geordie Heaerton; for taking 200 kie and oxen, 800 sheep and gaite, six horses and mares from Lunden.'

And…

'The Laird of Mangerton complains upon Mr Humfrey Musgrave, Captain Pikeman and his soldiers; for taking him prisoner; oxen, kie, horses, mares, sheep and gaite, insight value £1,500 sterling.'

Perhaps this last one was not upheld – Musgrave was the warden's man!

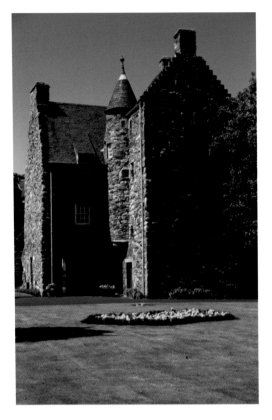

Mary, Queen of Scots House, Jedburgh.

The story goes that the Armstrongs' original name was 'Fairburn' and the change was brought about by a strange incident. The king is reputed to have asked Fairburn for help when mounting his horse. Fairburn reached out and, taking a grip on the king's thigh, heaved him effortlessly into the saddle. Henceforth, it was decreed he would be known by the name of 'Armstrong'.

Mary, Queen of Scots House, Jedburgh

Mary, Queen of Scots stayed in Jedburgh during 1566 when she was presiding over the assize courts, traditionally administering justice to various Reivers who had broken the law.

At this time James Hepburn, the Earl of Bothwell, resided in Hermitage Castle when he held the position of Lord of All the Scottish Marches, and he suffered a nasty encounter with the most notorious Reiver, Little Jock Elliot. Bothwell came off worse, and indeed he was in danger of dying from the wound inflicted by Little Jock's dagger. Mary, Queen of Scots heard of his terrible plight and rode the 30 miles from Jedburgh on horseback to see him and returned on the same day. She had travelled almost 60 miles across some of the most remote and wild country in the Borders in the cold and wet October weather. She took gravely ill on her return and lay for nine days in a small upper room in the turret. Lord Darnley, her husband, visited her and was greatly concerned, even though their relationship had started to cool by this time. Her fever raged – she even lost her sight at one stage – and eventually she lay so rigid and cold that her attendants assumed she was very close to death and even opened the windows in keeping with the superstition of the times. Mourning dresses were ordered and the arrangements made for the funeral; the Earl of Moray even started putting her jewels and silver plate to one side for himself. However, the Royal patient recovered and was able to leave Jedburgh a couple of weeks later for Kelso to preside over another assize court. She and her entourage were accompanied on the journey by the Earl of Bothwell, who, of course, was to eventually become Mary's third husband.

During the return ride from Hermitage the Queen's horse became bogged down and she was thrown – at a place now named the 'Queen's Mire'. In a desperate struggle to free herself from her awful predicament, she lost her watch. It lay buried for almost 250 years until the bog was drained and it was found by a shepherd, probably brought to the surface by burrowing moles or rabbits, but found to be in excellent condition, preserved by the peaty soil. It is now on display in the house along with a spur that was found nearby which could have also belonged to the queen or one of her party.

At the time of her visit the house was only about 20 years old, as were most of the houses in the town, which had been devastated 50 years previously by the Earl of Surrey in his unstoppable rampage after the Battle of Flodden. It was built as a bastle house in 1523 by Andrew Kerr of nearby Ferniehirst, traditionally with a left-handed staircase to suit the Kerrs. Some historians believe it was built specially for the queen's use, but whichever it is it still had the distinction of being one of the few houses in Jedburgh with indoor sanitation.

Melrose Abbey

Melrose is possibly Scotland's best known Abbey and is the successor to the seventh-century community which St Cuthbert joined at Old Melrose, about two miles away. The present abbey was founded in 1136 by King David I, who brought a group of Cistercian monks here from Rievaulx Abbey, near Helmsley, in North Yorkshire. This was the first Cistercian Abbey in Scotland, but because of their popularity King David founded another four of their houses in Scotland.

Because it was so close to the border, Melrose often suffered attacks by English Armies. In 1322 Edward II desecrated and burned the abbey – he ruthlessly killed Abbot Peebles – a

Melrose Abbey.

great friend of Robert the Bruce, along with many of his monks, in revenge for the scorched earth policy the Scots had adopted. In 1326 Robert the Bruce had awarded the abbey £2,000 for its rebuilding and maintenance, but in a repeat act of sacrilege in 1385 it was destroyed again by Richard II and his rampaging army. The offence was inevitably repeated by the Earl of Hertford in 1545 – it seems that English Monarchs and their nobility took a perverse delight in destroying the sacred edifices of Scotland – and did so with unrestrained vigour. In the years leading up to the attack by Henry VIII's army there were 130 monks at Melrose, but it was never to recover after the devastation of 1544, and at the Reformation in 1560 there were only 20 monks at the Abbey. Thirteen were pensioned off and the others took up new posts in the new Protestant church.

It was at Melrose that the heart of Robert the Bruce was buried. The story tells that when he was on his deathbed Bruce asked his good friend and colleague Sir James Douglas to remove his heart from his body after his death and carry it into battle on a crusade against the Infidel. After that he asked for his heart to be buried at Melrose and his body to be buried at Dunfermline beside that of his queen, Elizabeth de Burgh. Bruce's wish was carried out, but Douglas was killed on the crusade – faced with impossible odds he flung the heart into the battle and bravely followed it to his death. The heart was recovered and brought to Melrose where it was buried in the abbey under the east window of the chancel.

Another notable character buried in Melrose is Michael Scott, the wizard. His parents were from the Borders, but some say he was born in Fife; others say that he was born in Durham. He is variously known as a wizard, an alchemist, a necromancer, an astrologer and as a possessor of secret knowledge and great power.

In fact, he was one of the most intelligent, well educated and much travelled men of his time. He was highly regarded enough to have been advisor to two popes and Astrologer Royal to Frederick II, the Holy Roman Emperor. He also took up the study of medicine and gained a great reputation in that profession. He is said to have predicted his own death in 1236 by being hit by masonry falling from a church, and consequently all his life he wore a metal helmet in an attempt to cheat fate. He came to England where he found favour and respect at court and was knighted by Edward I.

Eventually, he returned to Scotland and it was here, some historians believe, that he died. He had a great reputation as a wizard and a magician, rather than as an academic, a scientist and a philosopher as he was known in other countries. His reputation as a necromancer was enhanced by Dante and James Hogg – the Ettrick Shepherd – and, of course, by Sir Walter Scott, who wrote about him in *The Lay of the Last Minstrel*. With the eye ever on a good legend, Sir Walter claims his namesake was buried 'on a night of woe and dread' in Melrose Abbey, along with his mighty book of spells and wizardry in the same grave. For many, many years naughty children were frightened with a sinister 'Auld Michael will get ye…'

Muckle Mouthed Meg

In the early 1600s Young Willie Scott lived at Dryhope Tower overlooking St Mary's Loch

Muckle Mouthed Meg sculpture.

in the Yarrow Valley with his family. He was a fine looking young fellow who commanded great respect from his peers. Of course, he did get up to a bit of 'lifting by moonlight' now and again, in common with most men in the Borders in those days – the trick was not to get caught in the act. Unfortunately for young Willie, he did get caught, and it could not have been worse. He was apprehended during a daring raid on Elibank Castle, the home of Sir Gideon Murray, who was the king's privy councillor and, indeed, a renowned keeper of excellent cattle, which was probably the very thing that had tempted young Willie in the first place. Willie was thrown into the dungeon with the promise that the next day he would be hanged for his crime.

Lady Murray was absolutely horrified – what a waste of a fine looking young man, especially when she had three daughters at home. It did not take her long to work out that young Willie would make a fine match for her eldest, poor Meg, whose muckle mou'

(large mouth) had made her too ugly to find a suitable husband thus far. She put the idea to Sir Gideon, and he did the decent thing by offering Willie the opportunity to marry Meg or go to the gallows…

Some say he asked for three days to think about it; others say he jumped at the chance; however, the outcome was that they did marry and the marriage was a long and happy one.

Naworth Castle, Brampton

Naworth Castle, near Brampton, holds pride of place on the western side of the Borders. One of the most famous people associated with the castle is Lord William Howard, or Belted Will as he is perhaps better known. However, he did not come into the estate until the Union of the Crowns but obviously its colourful history predates that time.

It was during the time of the Dacres that the castle most served the purpose for which

Naworth Castle.

it had been built, that is 'to defend the countrie and annoye the enemye'. It has been suggested that Gospatric, Earl of Northumberland, had a hall on this site in the early 1200s, although it was most probably built of timber. However, it was in 1335 that Ranulph de Dacre obtained a licence to crenellate his house at Naworth from Edward III, which he did by adding a tower and enclosing the courtyard with a substantial stone wall. It was Thomas, Lord Dacre, who distinguished himself at the Battle of Flodden and served as warden of the English West March for Henry VIII, who carried out further improvements with the addition of the Great Hall and what is now known as 'Lord Williams Tower'.

The reign of the Dacre family came to an end in 1560 when the then Lord Dacre died, leaving a widow, three daughters and a young son called George. Thomas Howard, the 4th Duke of Norfolk, married the widowed Lady Dacre and arranged for his three sons to marry her three daughters. Unfortunately,

young George was killed in a fall from a vaulting horse and the vast Dacre estates passed into the control of the Howard family. After his wife died Thomas Howard became involved in an ill-fated plot whereby he would marry Mary, Queen of Scots. However, the plot failed and when he was imprisoned and executed in 1572 a furious Queen Elizabeth seized his lands and titles.

The Dukes third son, Lord William Howard, married Elizabeth, the eldest Dacre daughter, and by 1602 he had raised the money to pay the ransom of £10,000 to regain his wife's estate. He set about extensively restoring the castle. He was a well-educated and honourable man and was responsible for maintaining the law in the area for both James I and his son Charles I. It is said that there are the remains of an old oak tree in the grounds of Naworth where Lord William had Reivers and criminals hanged, and reputedly over 60 Armstrongs were hanged over a period of two years.

Today the castle is owned by Philip and

Elizabeth Howard, and although it is not generally open to the public they make it and the 2,000-acre estate available for special exclusive events such as car launches, country pursuits, film locations, private historical tours and weddings.

Neidpath Castle, Peebles

Neidpath Castle, originally known as 'Jedderfield', lies about a mile to the west of Peebles and was built in the 14th century by Sir William de Haya or Hays, Sheriff of Peebles, replacing an earlier tower which belonged to the Fraser family. The Hays retained ownership of the castle until 1686 when it was sold to the Duke of Queensbury who gave it to his son the Earl of March. It is now privately owned by the Earl of Wemyss but is available to hire for functions. Mary, Queen of Scots visited the castle in 1563 on her third progress through her realm. William Hay, Lord of Neidpath, was a great supporter of the queen, and he also entertained her son, James VI, on his visit in 1586. The eerie prison chamber in the basement of the castle is last recorded as being used on 4 July 1594.

The castle is reputedly haunted by the forlorn 'Maid of Neidpath'. The Hays, while they were Earls of March, had their principal seat at Dunbar but often retired to Neidpath to enjoy the peace and tranquillity. Legend has it that the beautiful heiress to Dunbar and Neidpath fell in love with the young Laird of Tushielaw, from Ettrick Forest. The Scotts of Tushielaw were an honourable family but established their reputation in Border warfare and reiving. When the earl found out about their relationship he was furious because, in his opinion, the young laird was not suitable for his daughter, and he immediately put a stop to their meetings. The young laird was so distressed that he left the country and his true love. She was inconsolable, pined for his company and

Neidpath Castle.

Niedpath Castle.

became frail and emaciated. The earl was extremely concerned about his daughter's health and changed his mind about their being together. News soon reached the young man, and he landed on the east coast and quickly rode 'with loose rein and bloody spur' to meet his loved one. Meanwhile, young Lady Hay thought she would surprise him by meeting him at the family home in Peebles, which he had to pass on his way to Neidpath. She sat patiently by the balcony to await his arrival, and soon she heard his horse approaching and rushed onto the balcony to greet him. She saw him approach, but to her great horror he did not recognise her and thundered straight past. She thought he no longer wanted her, and as she was very weak she died of a broken heart.

It is said that the ghost of the Maid of Neidpath can be heard in the castle softly crying as she glides from room to room searching for her lost young Laird of Tushielaw.

Newcastleton.

Newcastleton and Liddesdale

Newcastleton is the biggest village in Liddesdale and lies very near the English border. For hundreds of years it was in the front line of the constant skirmish and war between England and Scotland, and even after the Union of the Crowns in 1603 it was still the haunt of itinerant thieves and mosstroopers. The settlement originally grew up around Liddel Castle, built in the 11th century by Ranulph de Soulis, the Lord of Liddesdale. In fact, it was from this that the village took its name. Records tell us that the castle was a ruin by the 1600s, and by 1700 the settlement had spread further south and had taken the name Copyhaugh, from which Newcastleton takes its alternative name of Copshaw Holm. In 1793 the Duke of Buccleuch built a model village to a geometric plan, conveniently close to Liddel Water, which was to become established as the centre of the hand-weaving industry.

Towards the head of Liddesdale is the place where the Elliots and the Nixons lived; farmhouses have now replaced their towers at Redheugh, Hartsgarth and Lariston. Towards the south of the dale were the habitations of the Grahams and the Armstrongs, while towards the east is where the English clans of the Nobles, the Routledges and the Fosters, lived and bore the brunt of those fierce Scottish raids. Reiving was part of the natural character of most of the inhabitants of the border line from the Solway firth to Berwick, but it was in Liddesdale where it was finely honed into a well-organised system. This area was thick with Border pele towers – there were reported to be well over 80. They were

Liddesdale.

Minholm Cross

usually built in a position of natural strength, to make them easily defendable, close to the banks of a stream or river, high on a rocky outcrop or surrounded by woods and marshes. Such was the lawlessness of Liddesdale that it had its own 'Keeper', garrisoned in the most grim of the Border strongholds, Hermitage Castle.

Liddesdale was home to two of the main reiving families, the Elliots and the Armstrongs. The Laird of Redheugh was head of the Elliots and the Laird of Mangerton the head of the Armstrongs. The Reverend Borland, Minister of Yarrow, sums them up admirably in his *Border Raids and Reivers*: 'Both families were, without exception, notorious freebooters. Reiving was the business of their lives. They were inspired, if not with a noble, at least with an overmastering enthusiasm for their nefarious calling.

'They were strongly of the opinion that all property was common by the law of nature

and that the greater thief was the man who had the presumption to call anything his own!'

This was, no doubt, an uncomplicated doctrine, but the consequences of its application simply served to cause further

Ettleton Kirkyard.

raid and reprisal. There is a story of a woman who was unsuccessfully seeking shelter in Liddesdale and in desperation asked 'Are there no Christians here?' to which came the blunt reply 'Na we're all Elliots and Armstrongs!'

By 1552, after the dispute over the Debateable Land was settled, the English lived in such great terror of the men of Liddesdale that the March warden ordered constant watches to be kept – this took over 60 men plus a number of 'largg dogges' – at one time there were over nine slewe dogs kept at one place in case of raids.

About a mile to the south of Newcastleton is the Milnholm Cross. One of the Armstrongs' most valued ancient relics, it commemorates the murder of Alexander Armstrong, the Second Laird of Mangerton, by one of the notorious de Soulis family. It marks the spot where his body was laid when it was brought from Hermitage, and some historians believe he is buried beneath the monument.

Just up the road past the cross is Ettleton Cemetery, where there are many interesting headstones of local families – many Reiver names among them including Elliot, Crozier, Oliver, Potts and, of course, Armstrong. Appropriately, just across the valley are the remains of the Armstrong Tower of Mangerton.

Norham Castle

Probably more than any other castle in the north, Norham captures the imagination as a symbol of the Border wars. This mighty

The keep at Norham Castle.

fortress lies midway between Berwick and Coldstream and once guarded the most important ford on the River Tweed.

Norhamshire was not originally part of Northumberland but was an outpost of the County Palatine of Durham and the castle was the main border stronghold for the Prince Bishops of Durham, as opposed to the king.

The first castle on the site is thought to have been built by Bishop Ranulph Flambard in 1121, although it was probably a wooden tower built on a mound surrounded by a wooden palisade and a defensive moat.

It was Henry II who ordered the rebuilding of the more important border castles in stone. At that time Hugh Pudsey was Bishop of Durham, and he set about rebuilding Norham on a grand scale, including the addition of the great red sandstone keep which dominates the site.

Norham Castle stood for over 100 years, seemingly impregnable; a challenge to the Scots who, apart from a siege in 1215, seemed content to wait for an opportunity to present itself. The chance arose when Edward I died and left his inept son to lead England. The Scots were under the leadership of the powerful Robert the Bruce, and he was keen to put Norham to the test and brought a huge force across the Tweed to rush the fortress. However, it stood firm. Not one to give up easily, he made a second attempt the following year and this siege was to last almost seven months, but still the garrison held. Among the English defenders was a knight called Sir Walter Marmion, who provided the inspiration for the hero of Sir Walter Scott's epic poem. Scott wrote mainly of the events leading up to Flodden – about

Marmions Arch, West Gate, Norham Castle.

200 years later – but his use of poetic licence has moved Marmion to a more glamorous age.

For another 150 years the ownership of Norham was hotly disputed. It fell to Scottish hands in 1327 but was restored to the Bishop of Durham by the treaty of Edinburgh. During the Wars of the Roses it changed hands twice: Yorkist to Lancastrian and back to Yorkist. After the wars, the Tudors ordered the further strengthening of their border strongholds, which turned out to be a wise decision because in 1497 Norham was put under siege by James IV but held out for 16 days under Bishop Fox until it was relieved by the Earl of Surrey.

King James made another attempt to take Norham on 23 August 1513. On this occasion his favourite piece of ordnance 'Mons Meg' was used against the massive walls. At the end of a two-day bombardment the barbican was in ruins and the outer ward had been taken by assault; by 29 August Sir Richard Cholomley, the garrison commander, had surrendered. King James and his army went on to meet their fate at Flodden Field. After the battle, Bishop Ruthall repaired the damage done by the Scots and greatly strengthened the fortress using materials taken from his castle at Middleham.

In 1530 the Scots attacked Norham again, but it was successfully defended under Archdeacon Framklin, who was granted a coat of arms by Henry VIII for his bravery. Norham was used for defensive service right up until the Union of the Crowns, after which it gradually sank into the dramatic ruin we see today.

Otterburn Tower, Otterburn

Otterburn Tower is now a comfortable hotel but stands on the site of an old pele tower that

Otterburn Tower.

played a part in the Battle of Otterburn. On their way back from Newcastle to the border, the Scottish forces attempted to take it. They began their attack at dawn, but the pele was so strong and well defended, in what was then a marshy and difficult environment, their enthusiasm and stamina waned with their lack of success, and they retreated to their nearby overnight camp. Many of the Scottish leaders were in favour of continuing their journey home over the border, but they were over-ruled by the Earl of Douglas, who insisted the tower must be taken. However, before the next morning Harry Hotspur and his men arrived at Otterburn and the importance of taking the tower was forgotten.

At the beginning of the 1400s the tower passed into the possession of Sir Robert de Umfraville and thereafter into the ownership of the Halls – a large and powerful Redesdale clan who were feared and hated on both sides of the border. They were well noted for an act of betrayal and treachery against the Keeper of Redesdale: Parcy Reed was appointed Keeper of Redesdale and this upset the Halls, who felt they were the more important family and one of their own should have held the position. Reed's enthusiasm for his appointment also earned him the vehement hatred of the Crosers of Liddesdale. A plan began to unfold: the Halls had the motive to rid themselves of Reed, and the Crosers certainly had the means. The opportunity presented itself when Reed invited the Halls to go hunting with him. They eagerly accepted and invited him to their home to discuss the next day's sport over a meal. Reed failed to notice that the bread on the supper table was up-side down – a traditional sign of impending doom. While he was enjoying their hospitality, the Halls sabotaged his weapons. They dampened the powder in his gun and made sure his sword would be jammed in its scabbard, an old ploy was to pour in raw egg, which would dry, making it impossible to draw the sword.

The next day when the party stopped to feed and water their horses, high on the lonely fells, the Halls pointed out a party of approaching Crosers. Parcy Reed felt it was his duty to tackle them, but he was unable to draw his sword and his gun blew up when he fired it. 'They fell on him all at once and mangled him most cruellie…' In fact, he was so badly mangled that his remains were taken home wrapped in a sheet.

For many years after this incident the Halls were treated with doubt and suspicion. If they asked for hospitality – and were lucky enough to receive it – they would find the cheese placed up-side down on the table, a traditional sign of disrespect. Such was the Borderers' fear and horror of betrayal.

Preston Tower, Northumberland

Preston Tower was built in 1392 following similar designs to those of Langley Castle and Tarset Castle. Originally, it would have been a rectangular building with turrets at each of the four corners, but now only two of the turrets are left, along with the wall between them and some parts of the side walls. The stronghold is an old one and was one of a list of 78 border fortresses recorded in Northumberland in 1415 – the time of the Battle of Agincourt. At that time it was held by Robert Harbottle, who was a man of some importance. He was in royal favour, he had served as Sheriff of Northumberland and as Constable of the nearby Dunstanburgh Castle. Later it is mentioned as being held by Sir Guishard Harbottle, who was killed at the Battle of Flodden Field in 1513.

Unusually, the basement and the first floor of the south-west tower are vaulted and the door at the base is under 5ft high – no doubt

Preston Tower.

a legacy from a time when defence was all-important. The building is now a clock tower and the hours are struck on a bell that was cast in Newcastle. The house near to the tower is also called Preston Tower and was built in the early 1800s for Edmund Craster.

The present owner, Major Baker-Cresswell, has created several interesting displays and reconstructions to show different aspects of the lives of the Reivers and these, together with other items on show, related to Border history bring back the grim reality of what things were like in those days.

The Redeswire Fray – 7 July 1575

The main A68 road crosses the border at Carter Bar. It is a wild and desolate spot, but along the ridge, just out of sight to the east of the road, a stone monument known as 'The Redeswire Stane' marks the site of 'the Raid of The Redeswire', and some historians believe that the incident here was the last time that the Scots and English fought each other as national enemies.

A Wardens' Meeting or 'Day of Truce' was held here on 7 July 1575. Sir John Forster was the English warden and Sir John Carmichael, 'The Keeper of Liddesdale', represented the

Redeswire Stane.

Scots. Each man was accompanied by his retinue and a large group of armed men. Initially an atmosphere of congeniality and good humour prevailed, lending the proceedings the mood and appearance of a country fair – itinerant travellers set up their temporary booths and peddlers put their wares on sale. The first bills that were presented to the wardens were dealt with quickly and efficiently until one was presented by a Scottish Borderer against a notorious Northumbrian Reiver named Farnsteen. This is thought to be an unusual name for a Reiver, but perhaps it could have been linked with Fousteen, the old name for the Northumberland village of Falstone. However, the bill was 'fyled' and Carmichael demanded the delivery of the offender for immediate punishment. Forster claimed that the man had fled and could not be traced. Carmichael became indignant, some say downright offensive, calling Forster's integrity into question. And this was probably true; Forster was involved in several shady deals with known law-breakers, although it is doubtful if he was directly involved in the activities of the vanished Farnsteen. Carmichael 'raxed himself in the saddle' and further suggested that Forster was quick to put his own interests above those of justice. Forster replied with equally caustic comment and even pulled rank on the Scot who, as 'Keeper of Liddesdale', was not regarded as a full warden. The intensity of the arguments and insults escalated and the respective wardens' followers became enthusiastically involved in the altercation. Almost immediately, violence broke out – there would have been many men on either side that were already at feud and were just looking for an excuse for a fight, so it would be difficult to say who was to blame. The first casualties were Scots. This suggests that the Tynedale Bowmen with Forster fired the first volley. Carmichael and Forster tried desperately to stop the trouble but failed miserably.

At first the Scots got the worst of it and would have been completely routed but for two circumstances. Firstly, the Tynedale men, aware of their superior strength, began to rob the attending merchants and fell into serious disorder. Secondly, a group of well-armed Jedburgh men on their way to the Truce Day appeared on the scene. They were able to help mount a successful counter offensive and the skirmish turned into a resounding victory for the Scots. Several of the English were killed, including Sir George Heron, the English deputy warden. Sir John Forster, Cuthbert Collingwood, and Lord Francis Russell, Forster's son-in-law, were among those taken prisoner and they were held for a while in Dalkeith by the Earl of Morton. He soon sent them back to England, well treated and with gifts including some hunting falcons. This gave

rise to a tale on the Borders that says the Regent got the worst of the bargain by exchanging live hawks for dead herons – alluding to the death of Sir John Heron.

Queen Elizabeth was outraged at the event and demanded satisfaction. She sent the Earl of Huntingdon to Berwick to discuss the problem with the Earl of Morton. Morton made concessions in an attempt to heal the offence, and Carmichael was held responsible and was sent to York to stand trial. However, the English court was unable to come to a definite decision, and it was agreed that initially Forster had been as much to blame. The outcome was that Carmichael was sent home with a full pardon.

Although it cannot be regarded as one of the major Border battles, the Reedswire Fray serves as a reminder of the things that could, and did, go wrong on a Wardens' Truce Day. The inscription on the windswept Redeswire Stane describes it simply: 'On this ridge 7th July 1575 was fought one of the last Border frays, known as the Raid of the Redeswire.'

Repentance Tower.

Hoddom Castle, home of the Maxwells.

Repentance Tower, Ecclefechan, Dumfries and Galloway

Repentance Tower, near Ecclefechan in Dumfries, was built in the 1560s for Sir John Maxwell, 4th Lord Herries of Terregles, high on Trailtrow Hill just to the south of Hoddom Castle. From the tower there is a commanding view of the border, especially south to the Solway Firth and the River Esk where incoming raiding parties could easily be seen. The tower was a vital link in the Reiver warning system and a beacon would have been lit to warn of any enemy approach.

The unusual name, Repentance, has inspired numerous tales rich in legend as to why it was built, but, as the name would suggest, it was most likely to atone for some sinister act of betrayal.

Towards the end of the 1540s the English Army occupied Dumfriesshire at the time of 'the Rough Wooing', and many of the locals were forced to swear an oath to Henry VIII and became 'assured Scots' – and just to make sure the pledge was secured by the giving of hostages to the English. Among these assured Scots was John Maxwell. More than anything, at that time, he wanted to marry Agnes Herries of Terregles, but to do that meant breaking his oath. He did just that – he raised

an army, traditionally under a black flag, and turned against the English at the Battle of Durisdeer. The defeated English retreated to Carlisle where they executed all but one of the Maxwell hostages in revenge for him breaking his oath.

Sir John Maxwell married Agnes and with this came the title of Lord Herries and all the lands, but it was at great cost – sadly his kinsmen had paid with their lives.

Repentance stands at the edge of an old graveyard, near to the site of an old chapel owned by the Bishop of Glasgow. Maxwell felt it was appropriate to have his watchtower built from the old stones of this chapel. It would serve both as a lookout to defend Scotland and as a monument to those who had died when he broke his word to the English.

Roxburgh Castle, near Kelso

Just over a mile outside of Kelso the road to Melrose skirts the foot of a long high ridge, fringed with the remains of some broken walls. This is all that is left of what was possibly the most powerful castle in the Scottish Borders.

It is widely believed that there has been some sort of fortification on this naturally defendable site between the River Teviot and

Roxburgh Castle.

Roxburgh Castle.

the River Tweed since Saxon times, although in the 1100s it was the royal residence of King David I who worked hard to bring trade, prosperity and modern government to Scotland.

The castle was well situated to protect the prosperous town that had grown around its walls. The Royal burgh of Roxburgh had a city seal and its own mint and was second in importance only to Berwick. It was enclosed by an extensive defensive wall with several gates, one of which, no doubt, would have led to a bridge across the River Tweed. There were many houses, schools and two churches and just outside the walls was the convent of Grey Friars. The town was abandoned in favour of Kelso in the 16th century, but it seems almost impossible that such a busy town should have disappeared so completely.

After the Battle of Dunbar in 1296 the castle was surrendered to Edward I, and for almost 100 years the Scots repeatedly attacked the castle to try and regain possession – even William Wallace mounted an unsuccessful attempt to recapture it for Scotland.

In 1313 Sir James Douglas, 'the Good Sir James', as he was known, succeeded in capturing the castle by stealth and cunning with only 60 men. One Shrove Tuesday evening, in the gathering dusk, an English guard saw what he thought to be a herd of black cattle in the meadows below. Suspecting nothing, he continued his patrol. The 'black cattle' were Douglas's men, covered by their long black cloaks, creeping along the narrow path between the castle and the River Teviot. Quietly and quickly they scaled the walls and took the garrison by surprise – most of the English were killed in the attack, although the

captain and a handful of men held out in the keep for over a day.

However, after the battle of Homildon Hill in 1334 the castle was ceded to Edward III of England, only to be retaken shortly after by Sir Alexander Ramsey for King David II of Scotland, but he was captured at the Battle of Neville's Cross, Durham, in 1346 and the castle, once again, fell into English hands.

In 1346 King James II of Scotland led an assault on the castle, but he was killed during the siege when his great gun, 'The Lion', a dodgy primitive piece of Flemish ordnance, blew itself to pieces, taking him with it – not to be deterred the enraged Scots stormed the castle and it was 'doung tae the ground'.

By 1547 the English controlled the Borders once again, and the Earl of Hertford adapted and converted the castle ruins into an artillery fort. It was back in the hands of the Scots by 1551 but was eventually demolished as part of the conditions of a peace treaty between England and France.

Shittleheugh Bastle House, Otterburn

The remains of Shittleheugh Bastle House can be found two miles to the north of Otterburn in Redesdale. From its position there are extensive views, particularly towards Scotland, which would have been one possible direction of attack. The bastle stands almost at the crossroads of two ancient routeways – one led through Hopehead and on to Holystone and the other followed the Durtrees Burn – and no doubt these tracks would have been well used when the building was constructed about 400 years ago. From

the remains, it is obvious that Shittleheugh was a substantial building – the walls, built from huge blocks of stone, are over 4ft thick and still stand at between 4ft and 6ft in height and presumably the gable ends are still at full height. The whole building would have been built to two storeys and measured between 30ft and 40ft long and over 20ft wide. As usual with this type of building, the emphasis was very much on defence. The door frame is formed from seven massive stones and the windows are, in effect, loopholes with their jambs angled at about 45 degrees, which would have given a wider line of fire when under attack. Unusually for this type of building, the access to the upper floor seems to have been by a small staircase in a porch rather than the wooden ladder that was normally used – and also the door to the ground floor is situated in one of the long

sides, a feature only used on the 'more elaborate' bastles.

Shittleheugh is an inspiring place with its mesmerising panoramic views, especially towards those enigmatic Scottish Hills, and standing on the fellside it is easy to imagine the stealthy approach of a band of Reivers – the sound of their advance hardly discernible – mingled intangibly with the sound of the

Shittleheugh Bastle House, Otterburn.

A slewe hound would have been strong and fast.

wind whispering through the ancient remains of this atmospheric building.

Slewe Dogges

Slewe hounds or Slewe dogges, as they were called, were an important part of life in the Borders. After a successful raid thieves would attempt to drive their lifted livestock home as quickly as possible. If the hue and cry of Hot Trod was mounted it would have been impossible to pursue them through the treacherous bogs and mosses without a good hound to follow their tracks. Packs of hounds or, in some cases, individual dogs, were kept at strategic points along the border to assist in following the villains. Dogs were so highly valued that one law stated if anyone should 'obstruct a slewe dogge in the course if its duty' they would be condemned as an accessory to the theft. An earlier law in Scotland said that if any man should kill another's dog he would have to assume the said dog's guarding duties 'on the owner's midden' for a year and also be liable to pay the owner substantial financial compensation.

These dogs would be somewhat similar in size to a modern foxhound, being fit and fast with a good nose for a scent. They took their characteristic name from their excellent ability to follow a trail. Research has shown that they probably looked like a cross between a foxhound and a labrador with slightly larger ears, giving rise to their other name of 'lurg dogge' – a reference to their lugs or ears.

It was probably difficult to evade such enthusiastic pursuers, but there were two defences the Reivers regularly employed against the hounds: one was to slaughter one

Sandyknowe Farm.

of the animals they had stolen, hoping the dogs would stop and feed on the carcass, and the other was to ride down shallow rivers or streams to break the scent trail and stop the dogs.

There was another way to stop the Slewe dogges following the scent and that was to steal these highly-prized and very valuable animals. Such an incident is recorded as a complaint in an entry in the *Calendar of Border Papers* for 1590:

'Complaint against Will of The Steil, and his son, also Will, Andrew Carr and Robine Ellott [*sic*], and others – for stealing from Catton: 30 cow and oxen, 4 horses and mares and sundry prisoners, Cuthbert Rowl, Clement Troop and 15 others – ransoming them from 13s 4d to £5.00; taking their horses – 40s to £5.00 and a slewe dogge – £10.00! a sword and spear price 20s – six days after St Luke's Day 1589.'

The dog was valued at twice the price of a horse and, interestingly, much more than the ransom asked for the prisoners.

Smailholm Tower

Smailholm Tower is sited almost midway between Melrose and Kelso and once belonged to the Pringle family. In 1408 they are recorded as serving as squires to the

Smailholm Tower.

powerful Black Douglases who were crushed by King James II in 1455. The Pringles, in common with many Scottish families, were touched by the tragedy that was the Battle of Flodden; David Pringle and his four sons were all killed. During the mid-1500s Smailholm was repeatedly attacked and damaged by the English as they marched north. However, safety was secured in 1548 when the laird, John Pringle, swore allegiance as 'an assured Scot' – that is in return for his promise not to raid England or to oppose any English raiders in Scotland, and his family, property and lands would be left unharmed.

Smailholm remained in the possession of the Pringles until 1645 when it was sold to the Scotts of Harden. They moved to Sandyknowe in 1700 and the tower was left to become derelict.

As a boy Sir Walter Scott used to stay at Sandyknowe farmhouse, which was owned by his grandfather. The wonderfully romantic location and setting had a profound effect on the youngster and was to provide much inspiration for his future stories and ballads.

The tower is four-storeys high and is set on a rocky ridge and offers splendid panoramic views of the surrounding countryside. It houses an excellent display of models, paintings and tapestries illustrating many of the Border tales and ballads.

Queen of the fairies exhibit, Smailholm Tower.

Smailholm Tower.

*Long pack,
Bellingham.*

St Cuthbert's Church, Bellingham, Northumberland

St Cuthbert's Church, Bellingham, was named in the traditional way of marking a temporary resting place of the saint's body on its epic journey from Lindisfarne to Durham. The first building on the site was probably constructed from wood and was replaced sometime around the beginning of the 12th century by the present church, built in the Norman style. Extremely strong

*Charlton window,
Bellingham.*

in construction, most of the exterior of the building still stands today. It is one of the few churches in England to have such a massive stone roof; this, however, dates from the 1600s and has alternate vertical rows of single and double thickness stone slabs, after the earlier wooden version had been twice burned by marauding Scots. The narrow chancel windows echo this necessity for defence. Not that Scots were the only problem – in the early 1500s a group of Charltons forced their way into the church and made the priest hold communion for themselves and several of their outlawed relatives. As time went on, things got no better and in the late 1500s 60 riders from the Scottish West March spoyled Bellingham on the day of St Cuthbert's Fair, and although much of what they took was recovered by Hot Trod they still managed to hang on to a fair amount of insight and several good horses. In 1597 the almost legendary Walter Scott of Harden raided Bellingham with 300 of his best riders. They killed three men and made off with over 400 head of livestock. The villagers could only hide in the church until it was over. There was no pursuit or redress in this case, much to the admitted shame of the warden.

By the early 1600s all this violence and raiding had taken its toll, and according to the records of the Dean and Chapter of Durham the church was attracting no support from the locals, communion was only held once a year, the font was badly damaged and the Bible, Prayer Book and Psalters were missing, and, to add insult to injury, the cleric could neither read nor write.

St Cuthbert's Church, Corsenside

The early Norman Church of St Cuthbert at Cosenside is in a solitary and exposed position but was once the centre of a small village, right up until the mid-1700s. It stands high above the River Rede near to what was the main Roman road of Dere Street, which linked York with southern Scotland. The church was very strongly built with thick walls and a heavy stone roof. Originally, the walls would have been pierced with small slit windows, but these were enlarged and altered to allow more light into the interior in the 1800s.

The church would have been the strongest building in the village and some historians believe it was used by the local people during Reivers' raids. Although there is no pele tower incorporated into its fabric, the thick walls and the small windows would have made the building more easily defendable, ensuring safety and protection for those who sought refuge.

St John's Church, Newton Arlosh, Cumbria

The name Newton Arlosh means 'New Town on the Marsh' and was established after the nearby village of Skinburness suffered severe

Holme Cultram Abbey.

damage from the sea during a violent storm in the 14th century. It was the monks of the nearby Holme Cultram Abbey who built the church in 1303; however, these unsettled times dictated that the building had to be easily defendable, and St John's is a fine example of a fortified church built during those turbulent times. The walls are over 6ft thick and the main doorway is only 2ft 7in wide, while the east window, the most important in any church, is only 11 inches wide. This church pele tower would have provided safety for the priest, the villagers and their animals during the frequent Scottish raids.

Tarras Moss

Tarras Moss was an extensive wasteland of treacherous bog, low scrub and dark woodland – it was used to great advantage by bands of Reivers seeking refuge or a safe hiding place. The moss was criss-crossed with safe pathways, but these were only known to those familiar with the terrain, and to an outsider it was a place of great danger, not only because of the dangerous peat bogs and the deep concealed pools but also from hostile prowlers.

Most of the mosses have now been drained, but one or two examples of this strange, unsettling landscape still exist. Tarras Moss, east of Hermitage Castle, was probably the largest, but there was also Spadeadam Wastes to the north of Gilsland and the huge expanse of the Solway Moss, which was not drained until the 18th century.

Interestingly, after King James's 'Pacification of the Borders' there were a few bands of Reivers following the old ways. They became known as 'Mosstroopers', possibly from their habit of seeking safety in the mosses but venturing out for raids and robbery.

Sir Robert Carey held both the positions of warden of the East English March and warden of the West English March during the

Tarras Moss was a treacherous place.

last 10 years of the reign of Queen Elizabeth I. A feud between the Ridleys and the Armstrongs, coupled with repeated raids on Haltwhistle, and the promise of more to come – the Armstrongs making 'bloody vows of deep revenge' – struck great fear into the hearts of Carey's subjects.

In the face of this, he made a plan to settle with the Liddesdale outlaws once and for all. Carey, with his deputies and about 150 horsemen, went up to the border and built a small fort. They laid in supplies and settled down to wait for any incursions. The outlaws responded by withdrawing into Tarras Moss with all their goods, and they too settled down to wait – for Carey's withdrawal.

Carey notes in his memoirs that 'the Tarras Wilderness was of great safety, and so surrounded by bogges and marshi ground with thick bushes and shrubbes, that they fear no power of England or Scotland'. He goes on to say 'They sent me word that I was like the first puff of a haggis, hottest at first, and bade me stay there as long as the weather would give me leave; they would stay in Tarras Wood until I was weary of lying in the waste and they no whit the worse.'

Carey's followers shared the Armstrongs' belief that Tarras Moss was impregnable, but he was determined to prove them wrong. During darkness he secretly sent an advance guard of 150 riders 30 miles into the moss, guided by 'a moffled man, not known to any of the companie'.

This force quietly split up to guard the three exits from the Tarras Moss, and at first light Carey attacked with over 300 horsemen and 1,000 foot leveys he had secretly assembled. The plan worked – the ambushes were sprung and most of the outlaw leaders

Tarras Moss has changed considerably since the 15th century.

were captured, and he was also able to obtain the release of many English prisoners and secure the submission of the rest of the outlaws, who gave themselves up the next day. He immediately released the Armstrongs he had captured. Pleased with a job well done, he wrote that 'he was never after troubled with this kind of people.' Although, it has to be said, others were…but only for a while.

There is an amusing story that says while Carey was patiently waiting for the Armstrongs they sneaked out of Tarras Moss and stole his cattle – to add insult to injury they allegedly sold them back to him to feed his troops.

Much of the Moss has now been drained and cleared.

Tarset Castle.

Tarset Castle, Northumberland

The huge green mound that is all that is visible of Tarset Castle stands on private land above the junction of the Tarset Burn and the North Tyne. It was built by a Scottish knight, John Comyn, Lord of Badenoch, who was also known as 'the Black Comyn'. It was his son, also John, 'The Red Comyn', who was assassinated by his rival to the Scottish Throne, Robert the Bruce, in Greyfriars Kirk in Dumfries in February 1306, who in this one action made himself owner of Tarset and took one step closer to the throne.

During the early 1500s the castle housed an English garrison whose unenviable task was to control the reiving families of the surrounding valleys.

In 1526 Sir Ralph Fenwick and 80 riders were sent by the March warden to arrest

Tarset Castle.

William Ridley, an outlaw who was known to have been involved in the murder of the High Sheriff, Sir Albany Featherstonehaugh (Fanshaw). The locals, however, did not care for Fenwick or his men, after all their loyalties lay with Ridley. Subsequently, a large force of Tynedale men, led by Sir William Charlton of Bellingham, with the help of several riders from Liddesdale, set about Sir Fenwick and his men and drove them out of Tynedale – just to emphasise their point they burned Tarset to the ground but, despite its strategic position, it was never rebuilt.

The Battle of Dryfe Sands, Lockerbie – 6 December 1593

Deadly feud was something that was ever present in the Borders, and possibly the greatest of these disputes was between the two great Dumfriesshire surnames: the Maxwells of Nithsdale and the Johnstones of Annandale. Although their names were occasionally mentioned in complaints in the *Calendar of Border Papers* neither seems to have been particularly worried about raiding into England. It was the rivalry between the heads of these two families that

Dryfe Sands near Lockerbie.

mainly occupied their attention – a situation that was made much worse by successive kings and regents rewarding each in turn with the position of warden of the Scottish West March – much to the considerable distaste and irritation of the other.

When James Douglas, Earl of Morton, was executed in 1581 his estates and title passed into the possession of John, Lord Maxwell, but instead of being content with his good fortune he put his new position at risk by using the power it gave him to enrich himself and his family rather than suffer the inconvenience of trying to keep order. Completely ignoring his obligations as warden, Maxwell gathered an army, its ranks swelled by a motley assortment of Armstrongs, Grahams and broken men of both countries, and set off to plunder Ettrick Forest. During the indiscriminate pillaging and plundering, he captured Adam Scott and Thomas Dalgleish – he

put them both in shackles and it is thought he chained Dalgleish to a tree – and held them both to what he thought would be a huge ransom. As a result of these activities, Maxwell was summoned to appear before the Privy Council, but he declined the opportunity and was therefore 'put to the horn' (outlawed) and as a result he lost his position and, predictably, a Johnstone was appointed in his place.

Maxwell continued his lawless activities but made the mistake of antagonising the king's favourite, the Earl of Arran, who immediately asked James for help. The king ordered Johnstone, the new warden, to arrest Maxwell and sent a troop of soldiers from Edinburgh to help in the operation, but they were soundly defeated and wiped out at Crawfordmuir by Maxwell's half brother. A highly-infuriated Robert Maxwell launched a savage attack on the Johnstones and burned their castle of Lochwood 'to give Lady

Johnstone light enough to set on her hood'. The Maxwells burned a further 300 houses and stole over 3,000 sheep from the Johnstones. Johnstone complained bitterly to the king that following orders had cost him over 100,000 crowns.

However, the Johnstones attempted to make good their losses in the traditional Border manner and twice attempted to attack Dumfries but were beaten by bad weather. However, it did not stop Maxwell from launching further retaliation. Eventually, it all became too much for Lord Johnstone and he died – some say of a broken heart – and the king was forced to find another warden. Inevitably he appointed a Maxwell to the position, but neither of these two hotly feuding families would have accepted an outsider in the office and the king did stipulate that they

Lochwood Tower, home of the Johnstones of Annandale.

should forget their grievances, which to an extent they did.

The whole situation soon flared up again. William Johnstone, 'the Gilliard', as he was known, raided the Crichtons – close associates of the Maxwells – who immediately retaliated by stringing him up from the nearest tree. Retribution was hard and swift. The Johnstones rode into Nithsdale and devastated everything in sight, leaving a trail of total destruction. In utter despair, a group of women from Nithsdale travelled to Edinburgh, taking with them 15 blood-stained shirts from the bodies of their murdered husbands. Neither the king or the council would listen to their plea for help, and so they took their protest to the streets of Edinburgh. The sight of these pathetic blood-stained shirts caused such outrage with the public that the king was forced to take action. He ordered the warden, Maxwell, to arrest Johnstone, and if he would not surrender he was to attack his castle at Lochwood 'and raze out the memory of him and his name in these bounds.'

Maxwell, with 2,000 men, arrived in Annandale with the specific intention of carrying out the kings orders to the letter. He offered a reward of 10 pounds' worth of land to anyone who brought him Johnstone's head or hand. Not to be outdone, but being less wealthy, Johnstone made a counter offer of five pounds' worth of land to anyone who brought him a piece of Maxwell.

Lord Maxwell reached the point not far from the town of Lockerbie near the confluence of the Rivers Annan and Dryfe, and he found the Johnstones waiting for him. Of course, Sir James, chief of the Johnstones, had been forewarned of Maxwell's approach and had called for urgent help, which was answered by the Grahams, Armstrongs, Scotts, Carruthers, Irvings, Elliots and their associates, including Robert Johnstone of Raecleuch who was only 11 years old.

Although Johnstone was heavily outnumbered, he was an experienced and cunning Border fighter and lured Maxwell's vanguard into a trap using the old ploy of feigning retreat. Just when the Maxwells thought they had the advantage, the main body of the Johnstone's force attacked, throwing their enemies into total confusion. Some of the Maxwells were even pursued through the streets of Lockerbie. The mixture of cavalry and infantry resulted in a large number of those on foot – particularly those who had been unmounted – suffering a particularly nasty downward blow with a sword to the face, rather than the usual leg injuries – these particular injuries became known by the rather dubious name of 'Lockerbie Licks'.

Maxwell himself was knocked off his horse, and being a particularly tall man and weighed down with his armour he could not stand up and was left for dead. There are two differing stories about his end. One version tells how Willy Johnstone, the 'Gilliard's' nephew, cut off Maxwell's arm when he raised it in a gesture of surrender and then killed him. The other story has it that Willy only cut off Maxwell's arm after he had died, and it was Lady Johnstone of Kirchill who brained him with the tower keys that hung on her girdle.

Whichever way he died, it seems that his arm was taken away as a trophy and nailed to the door of Lochwood Tower. The Battle of Dryfe Sands was not really conclusive because it settled nothing and the feud dragged on for another 15 years.

However, in 1608 a meeting to discuss a settlement of the dispute was arranged between Sir James Johnstone and Lord Maxwell, son of the chief who was killed at Dryfe Sands. The meeting was to be carefully supervised and each man was allowed only one attendant, but during the meeting an argument flared between the two attendants – it was probably pre-arranged – and this presented the opportunity for Maxwell to shoot Johnstone twice, in the back.

Maxwell immediately escaped and fled to France where he kept low for four years. However, on his return he was betrayed and taken to Edinburgh under close arrest where he was publicly beheaded.

The Battle of Solway Moss – 24 November 1542

In October 1542 the English Army, under the command of the Duke of Norfolk, advanced along the valley of the River Tweed. Roxburgh, Kelso and the abbey and more than a dozen other towns were destroyed and put to the fire. Meanwhile, the Earl of Hertford raided Teviotdale with over 2,000 riders, just to add to the devastation – all this

Solway Moss from Aurthuret churchyard.

Solway Moss.

fire and destruction would probably be satisfying to King Henry in the absence of any actual conquest.

While Norfolk's army was concentrating on the Eastern March, the Western March was left wide open to invasion. James V took advantage of this opportunity and his army, raised in the main by Lord Maxwell, was advancing. Maxwell was never officially in command – James had intended to lead the army himself but had taken ill and was forced to remain at Lochmaben while his forces, numbering about 18,000 men, advanced menacingly on the frontier and the city of Carlisle.

However, the warden of the English West March, Lord Wharton, was an experienced soldier and a shrewd commander. And, although the situation looked desperate, he chose to ride out with his competent and most able deputy, William Musgrave, and about 3,000 lances to meet the enemy instead of remaining in the safety of Carlisle Castle.

Musgrave was ordered to harass the enemy with his 'prickers' – the light horsemen who could make lightning attacks on the flanks of the Scottish Army – and then withdraw just as quickly. It was the kind of work that suited these skilful Border Riders. It was during these attacks that the Scots found themselves without a leader: Sir Oliver Sinclair, a favourite of King James, declared himself to be James's chosen commander, but the other commanders refused to accept his authority and consequently no decisive orders were given. No doubt if Maxwell had been in charge things would have been different, but the king did not trust him and it was not to be.

Wharton knew nothing of this, but he fought the battle to the best of his ability using his Reivers' perception and Reivers' tactics – his men were holding the frontier against a large army by charging and retreating, hitting and running. Eventually, and possibly through having no direct line of command, the Scottish Army began to crumble at the edges. Musgrave's riders kept on the pressure – riding their ponies into the very centre of the Scottish troops, and as they gave up the Reivers rode over them. The rout was complete. A few gallant 'prickers' had defeated a force at least four times greater than themselves.

Wharton estimated that he had lost seven men and one was taken prisoner. The Scottish losses are unknown but some historians believe over 1,000 men were taken prisoner and several hundred were killed, either by the English or in the treacherous bogs of Solway Moss.

The remains of the Scottish Army, fleeing northwards, suffered further attacks by Scottish Borderers who were always on the lookout for plunder and prisoners, no matter which side they were on! The Riders of Liddesdale killed some of the fugitives, while the rest were stripped of horses, boots, spurs, doublets and clothing – many had to travel home wearing their hose and undergarments. It is said that some of the fleeing soldiers were so terrified they surrendered to groups of women.

King James was devastated by the defeat at Solway Moss, and he left the Borders seriously ill and utterly dejected. He travelled to Falkirk Palace where, sadly, within two weeks he died an awful death, raging and crying out in anguish. He was only 30 years old and left a daughter only six weeks old – she was to become Mary, Queen of Scots. Her nearest male relative was her great uncle, the King of England, Henry VIII.

The Bishop's Curse, the Cursing Stone, Carlisle

In 1525 the Archbishop of Glasgow, Gavin Dunbar, could not tolerate the behaviour of the Scottish Reivers any longer, and in his fury, and indeed his desperation, he laid upon them what was, and very probably still is, the

The Cursing Stone, Carlisle.

*The Cursing Stone,
the Millennium
Gallery, Carlisle.*

greatest Monition of Cursing that had ever been invoked. If he had only excommunicated them at least there was a chance that it could have been lifted, but with a curse or commination once it had been brought down upon them and started to take effect it could not, under any circumstances, be undone.

Once it was prepared, the archbishop had it read from every pulpit in his episcopate. It began 'Gude folks, hear my Lord Archbishop of Glasgow's Letters under his round seal…' It went on to bring down on its victims every unimaginable evil thing that had ever happened since the beginning of time. The curse was laid on every part of them, any actions they were involved in, everything they owned, everything they did and everyone associated with them. Just for good measure, every type of evil that had befallen anyone was also brought to descend upon them. Thunder and lightning was called down upon their heads and raging fires called up to consume them. The curse went on for 1,500 words and finally, just in case the Bishop had overlooked any misfortune and evil, he continued 'and finally I condemn them perpetually to the deep pit of hell – and there to remain with Lucifer and all his Fellows – and their bodies to the gallows on Burrow Moor, first to be hanged, then to be ripped and torn by dogs, swine and other wild beasts, abominable to all the world. And their candle goes from their sight as may their souls go from the face of God, and their good reputation from the world until they forbear their open sins, aforesaid, and rise from this terrible cursing and make satisfaction and penance.

'And may they be cast down into the deep pits of hell and there be consumed by the fires

of Lucifer and their brains tortured by a foul penance in eternity.'

It had no effect at all on the behaviour of the Reivers.

As part of their Millennium celebrations, the city of Carlisle commissioned the 'Cursing Stone', which is prominently displayed in their subterranean Millennium Gallery which runs under the road linking the Tullie House Museum and Carlisle Castle. The stone, of solid granite, weighs 14 tonnes and is carved with 383 words of the curse, running in horizontal lines around its circumference – a small red arrow marks where the narrative is continued to the line below. The work was created by artist Gordon Young, a native of the city, and appropriately he bears a 'riding surname'. The Cursing Stone is an interesting and significant addition to the city and recalls an important but wild and dangerous period in its long history.

However, at one time a school of thought in the city blamed the stone for a series of 'misfortunes of biblical proportions'. Floods, foot and mouth disease and many job losses were suffered, not to mention a run of poor performances by the football team; feelings were running so high at one time that it was proposed to remove and destroy the stone but, fortunately, it is still in position; however, it provides much food for thought and it is just possible that the ghosts of those who rode by moonlight all those years ago might still have an influence.

The Debatable Land and the Scots Dike

The area of land to the north of Carlisle and to the west of Gretna, bounded on the west by the River Sark and on the east by the Esk and Liddell, to the north by Tarras Moss and to the south by the Esk estuary, was the Debatable

Land. This troublesome strip measured just over 10 miles from north to south and was just over four miles wide; however, its ownership was hotly disputed by England and Scotland and was a constant source of trouble to both. The main problem arose from the fact that neither country would admit that it was owned by the other and consequently neither could hold the other responsible for the actions of the people who lived there. Naturally, this opportunity was not to be missed and it attracted most of the worst troublemakers in the Borders, creating a dangerous situation that led to an ever increasing round of conflict and violence. The wardens found that one way of dealing with the area was to devastate it, making it completely unfit and impossible for anyone to live there, and even though this was done on a regular basis the resilient inhabitants returned almost as quickly as they were driven out. It was mainly the Armstrongs who lived in the north of the Debateable Land and the

The Scots Dike.

The Scots Dike.

shall inhabit upon any part of the said Debateable Land, without any redress to be made to the same.'

In the same year, just to emphasise the point, the Scottish warden, Lord Maxwell, devastated the area, burning every building to the ground. There were those who thought that this approach would solve the problem, but since devastation had not provided a solution in the past the majority felt it was better to go ahead with the plan for division and commissioners were appointed to carry out the task.

Lord Wharton and Sir Thomas Challoner represented England and Sir James Douglas of Drumlanrig and Richard Maitland of Lethington looked after Scottish interests. Predictably an agreement was not reached without a difference of opinion and the French Ambassador, who was appointed to see fair play, settled the question by compromise.

The new frontier was marked by a ditch and a bank dug along an east to west line from the Sark to the Esk still marked on the map as 'The Scots Dike'. A square stone was set up at each end with the Arms of England on one side and the Arms of Scotland on the other. The dike was originally about 3ft or 4ft high and almost 12ft across; it would appear that the construction teams started from opposite ends and slightly lost their bearings because where they should have met in the middle the two ditches miss each other by some 20ft.

The decree was ratified in Jedburgh on 9 November 1540, and we are told that the Scottish High Treasurer paid £1.4s for a gold and silk cord to hang on the document.

It was hoped that the satisfactory division of the Debatable Land would put a stop to Border raiding, but it had no immediate effect

Grahams, under the leadership of the notorious Long Will Graham, who lived in the south, but numerous fugitives and 'broken men' were also attracted to the area and it rapidly became necessary to make an attempt to find a permanent solution to this ever-increasing problem.

In 1540 the English put forward an idea that would solve the problem by laying claim to the whole area; however, the Scots strongly disagreed and proposed that it should be divided between the two countries.

It was considered essential that dramatic action should be taken before the actual division was agreed, and in 1551 the wardens of both countries issued a proclamation to the effect that 'All Englishmen and Scottishmen after this proclamation is made shall be free to rob, burn, spoil, slay, murder and destroy all and every such person or persons, their bodies, buildings, goods and cattle as do remain, or

because the Liddesdale Reivers put paid to those new hopes with a renewed vigorous outbreak of their predatory expeditions which was to continue for the next 50 years.

At least the division of the Debatable Land represented a small step forward in the co-operation between the countries after the war of 1540.

The Lochmabenstane, Old Graitney, Gretna

The Lochmabenstane can be found about 300 yards from the shore line in a westerley direction along the coast from the mouth of the River Sark, not far from Old Graitney, near Gretna. A very imposing landmark, it stands almost 8ft in height with a circumference of nearly 19ft and weighs about 10 tons. There are several fascinating theories about its origin and purpose. Some historians believe it marks the place where Maben, an important ancient tribal leader, fell in battle and was buried in about AD600. Others believe it was originally part of an ancient Druids' stone circle, endowed with all the mysteries and superstitions of their religion. And some, perhaps more pragmatic, theorists say that is a glacial erratic, dumped incongruously by a previous ice age.

It is, without doubt, a landmark of great significance. It was a place where armies rallied, a mustering point for the troops of Dumfries and Galloway, and it stands directly on the invasion route between Brough-by-Sands on the English Side of the Solway and the Scottish ford of Sulwath. In 1398 there is a record of the Scots and English meeting here to exchange prisoners.

The wardens of the West Marches held their Days of Truce here with all the associated activities of bills of complaints, trials of the accused and executions of the guilty – many a hapless Border Reiver met his end here.

When it was not being used as a convenient place to meet to dispense justice, it would also serve as a trysting place for Reivers to gather with their associates before setting off for another raid.

October 1488 saw a battle fought here when the Douglasses defeated their old enemies the Percys in what was to become known as the Battle of Sark or by some as the Battle of Lochmabenstane.

The Sieur de la Bastie, Warden of the Scottish East March

In 1517, during the long minority of James V, the Regent Albany appointed the celebrated French knight, the gallant, handsome and

South of Duns.

Anthony Darcy exhibition, Drumlanrig's Tower, Hawick.

swaggering Anthony Darcy – the Sieur de la Bastie – warden of the Scottish East March. Albany had probably been influenced in his choice because he had spent a lot of time in France and, indeed, had a French wife. This was the beginning of the period of great French influence in Scotland that ended with Mary, Queen of Scots.

The Homes looked upon the position of warden as their own and took a dim view of de la Bastie's appointment. Nevertheless, he approached the job with great enthusiasm and diligence, but his idea of indiscriminate justice did not appeal to the Homes and they felt he had to be taught a lesson.

They arranged an ambush four miles south of Duns, near Fogo, but the Frenchman was well mounted and an excellent horseman and managed to escape. Not to be outdone, the Homes chased him through the town in full cry and using their greater local knowledge managed to drive him into a swampy area where his horse was overtaken.

The warden was pulled from his horse, abused and killed – his handsome head was cut off and hung from Home of Wedderburn's saddle by its long plaited tresses who rode with it back to Duns where he hung it on the Mercat Cross as a grim warning to all, including regents and kings, who might have the temerity to interfere with the Homes.

No one was ever punished for the crime.

Thirlwall Castle

Thirlwall Castle is situated about half a mile to the north of the attractive Northumbrian village of Greenhead. It guards the entrance to what became known as 'busy gap' in the 15th and 16th centuries, a route much favoured by Border Reivers. The castle is a fine example of a border stronghold and is thought to date from the beginning of the 14th century – the nearby Roman Fort of Carvoran provided a ready-made supply of dressed stone for its construction. It was here in 1306 that the Thirlwalls entertained Edward I while he was on one of his many forays into Scotland. The name 'thirl' is Scottish in origin and means 'a break in the wall'. It is thought that this may be the point where the Caledonians first broke through Hadrian's Wall.

In common with other border strongholds, Thirlwall was regularly raided; however, one raid had strange and far-reaching consequences. The warden, William, Lord Dacre, was making things very difficult for the inhabitants of Liddesdale and the Debateable Land, and so the Armstrongs and their associates formed a plan to get their revenge.

A mixed band of about 30 Nixons and Crosers crossed the border into Bewcastle and lifted a small herd of cattle from Thirlwall. For good measure, they also kidnapped one of Dacre's tenants before making for home at an unusually leisurely pace. Dacre alerted his men, and they were soon in the saddle in hot pursuit. They picked up the raiders trail near Bewcastle and tried to persuade the soldiers in the garrison there to join them on the hot trod, but they had kept a low profile when the alarm was first raised and they were still reluctant to help. Furthermore, what was also a little unsettling was the way that the band of Reivers were taking exactly the same route home as they had followed on the raid. However, the warden and his band showed no concern for these signs, they enjoyed the advantage of hugely superior numbers and they caught up with the Scots within a short distance of the border. Dacre's men were about to move in for the kill when they were suddenly ambushed by hundreds of Armstongs, Elliots, Nixons, Crosers and their associates – the warden's men surrendered

Thirlwall Castle.

immediately, but over a dozen of them were cut down on the spot and another 40 or so were taken prisoner. There was outrage and uproar at the ambush and both governments had to appoint commissioners to examine the affair.

They arrived at the conclusion that the damage done to either side was about even, but the Scots admitted that the blame probably lay with Liddesdale because its people were beyond their control. They

Thirlwall Castle.

therefore accepted the English proposal that in reality Liddesdale should be excluded from any peace treaty – and if the inhabitants should step out of line the English authorities could legally take revenge without any further repercussions. There was also a proposal to allow the Scots to do this in England if the occasion demanded, but there was no area out of control like Liddesdale and the situation did not arise.

The people of Liddesdale held this attitude by the Scottish government in great contempt. Towards the end of 1528, Sim 'the Laird' Armstrong had a meeting with the Earl of Northumberland to discuss the release of his recently arrested kinsman, Quentin Armstrong. During their meeting Armstrong spoke openly about his feelings. He criticised the Scots and indeed he insisted that King James and his government were useless, and he further suggested that there would be no peace in Scotland unless the King of England ruled there. He pointed out that their incompetence had allowed him and his men to devastate over 60 square miles of land and destroy over 30 churches. Sim Armstrong was a respected and important leader, rather more than just an itinerant robber, and it was he and Johnnie Armstrong who had brought the family to the height of its power. Not only could they put over 3,000 men in the saddle but these powerful and charismatic men could also influence the political balance in the Borders.

Although some historians believe that Sim the Laird's opinions may have been exaggerated by the English, his views are echoed in the behaviour of the Armstrongs. No group of Scottish families have collaborated with the English as much or as often as the Armstrongs, Elliots, Nixons and Crosers – it has been said that this was because of the negative attitude of the Scottish government toward them, but there is also the underlying trait in the Reiver character that would suggest this situation may have also suited their purpose.

Thirlwell also harbours a curious legend. It is said that an early Baron of Thirlwell brought a magnificent jewel-encrusted table back from the wars he fought in France but news of this great treasure spread far and wide. A band of Scottish raiders got wind of this and attacked the castle. The baron and his followers were all killed, but a thorough search revealed no treasure. It was known to be guarded by a mysterious dwarf, but he was nowhere to be found. Legend has it that at the height of the battle he threw the treasure into a well and then jumped in himself, using his supernatural powers to seal the opening. It is said that the well is still there to this day – guarded by a secret spell that can only be lifted by the only son of a widow…

Threave Castle, Castle Douglas

Threave Castle stands on a low, grass-covered island in the River Dee, about seven miles to the north of Kirkcudbright. Because of the easily defendable position, it is likely that Threave Island has been settled since earliest times, but it was Archibald the Grim, the 3rd Earl of Douglas, who built the castle in 1369, not long after he was created the Lord of Galloway. He earned the name 'Grim' from the English 'because of his countenance in weirfare [battle].'

It was King David II who honoured the Black Douglases because of their unswerving loyalty

Threave Castle.

to the Crown. For his involvement in fighting for the king, Archibald was created Lord of Galloway and given the position of warden of the Scottish West March. It was Archibald the Grim who carried out the first successful assault on Lochmaben Castle and drove the English out of the Scottish West March. He died at Threave on Christmas Eve 1400.

Archibald, the 4th Earl of Douglas, died in 1424 fighting for the French against the English, but his wife, Princess Margaret, continued to live in Threave until her death.

In 1444 the marriage between two cousins, Margaret, the Fair Maid of Galloway, and William, the 8th Earl of Douglas, united all the Douglas estates. Consequently, James II

Threave Castle.

and the Douglases were soon at variance and Douglas was murdered by James in Sterling Castle in 1452. William's younger brother James, the 9th Earl, married his brother's widow swearing to avenge his death. The trouble soon began and by the beginning of 1455 King James had started to destroy all the Douglas strongholds. By the middle of the year only Threave remained. A two-month siege ensued and during this time the king stayed at nearby Tongland Abbey so he could supervise operations. It looked as if the king and his army were in for a long wait, and he sent off to Linlithgow Palace for a huge gun. After great difficulty and hardship, it arrived but was not used. The garrison was persuaded to surrender – not under threat of heavy bombardment, but by offering payments and lands to some of those in command of the defences, a more subtle and amicable arrangement. James II visited Threave again in 1460 on his way to lay siege to Roxburgh Castle, where he was killed when a big gun exploded.

In 1526 Lord Johnny Maxwell was made Keeper of Threave and during his residence the castle, regarded as one of the key strongholds to the Scottish West March, played a significant part in the Border wars, and from 1544 to 1545 it was actually held by the Earl of Hertford's men for the English.

Maxwell's behaviour as March warden left a lot to be desired. He was encouraging the Armstongs to ride with him in his family feud against the Johnstones and his shady dealings with his opposite number were not going unnoticed.

Eventually, the Maxwells' deeply religious Catholic beliefs upset both Mary, Queen of Scots, and the regent. In 1588 they journeyed to Spain to support the Armada and on their return they were ordered to surrender all their castles including Threave.

Following the Union of the Crowns in 1603, Maxwell was arrested for failing to pay his taxes. Eventually the role of Threave as a border fortress declined.

The castle saw action for the last time when Lord Robert Maxwell held out against the Army of the Covenant, led by Lt Col. Home, in support of Charles I, for 13 weeks until the king himself wrote to Maxwell, authorising his surrender.

The island castle was never occupied again, and in 1913 Edward Gordon, the owner, turned it over to state care and it was then passed to the National Trust For Scotland while the castle itself is in the care of Historic Scotland.

Torthorwald Castle, Torthorwald, Dumfries

Torthorwald Castle dates from the 1400s and is sited on a 250ft hill overlooking Nithsdale. It has had a varied history and the first building on the site belonged to Sir David Torthorwald and then passed to Sir Duncan Kirkpatrick, and it was probably his decision to build a motte and bailey style castle on the site. It passed into the possession of the Carlyle family when Sir Duncan's daughter married Sir John Carlyle, and he subsequently became Lord Torthorwald. Their son, Sir William Carlyle, married Janet Maxwell, daughter of Robert Maxwell, the 3rd Earl of Caerlaverock. Eventually the castle was passed to William Douglas, the 3rd Earl of Drumlanrig.

Not surprisingly, there is a record from 1544 of the then Lord Carlyle attacking the castle in a raid against his own sister-in-law – such were the complex and intricate interwoven grudges and intrigue that grew from deadly feud in those days.

Even the architecture of the castle does not follow a prescribed plan – it is a rectangular tower with vaulted first floor and basement and in one corner a winding staircase leads to the upper floor – the most likely site of the original entrance. Various styles of construction seem to have been used, reflecting perhaps the changes of ownership and their changes of fortune.

Tosson Tower, Rothbury

Tosson Tower, at Great Tosson near Rothbury, was built in the 14th century as one of a line of defensive towers sited along the Coquet Valley. It once belonged to the Hepple family, and at the end of the 13th century when Hepple Tower was destroyed, possibly by Robert the Bruce, the Lords of Hepple moved their courts to Tosson, making it a place of great importance. However, the original purpose of the tower was to protect the village, and when

Torthorwald Castle.

Tosson Tower.

Triermain Castle.

Triermain Castle.

Lord Wharton was deputy warden of the March he established an organised warning system and a watch of two men had to be maintained every night.

The tower eventually passed to the ownership of Sir Robert Ogle, Sheriff of Northumberland, and was one of six he owned along the border. It was he who recaptured Wark Castle from Sir William Haliburton by leading his men into the castle through the kitchen sewer.

directions – for bands of Reivers going about their unlawful business. At one time the castle served as a valuable outpost for Lord Dacre, warden of the March, to keep an eye on the various comings and goings in the area. However, the building was described as being in poor condition by the 1580s and indeed there is a record of a raid on Tremain in the 1590s by Walter Scott of Harden and his men.

Triermain Castle, near Brampton, Cumbria

Stones plundered from Hadrian's Wall were used in the construction of Triermain Castle between Brampton and Gilsland in Cumbria. The licence to crenellate was granted by Edward III in the middle of the 14th century to Roland de Vaux, the Baron of Triermain, although it seems certain that there was a substantial house on the site prior to this date. Its position, on the edge of Spadeadam wastes just to the south of Bewcastle, dictated the necessity for strong fortification because this was one of the favourite routes – in both

They were accompanied on this occasion by a number of Elliots from Liddesdale and between them managed to drive off over 60 head of cattle.

The few remaining stone fragments of Tremain stand on a small mound. Originally the castle was square in plan with towers on the east and west sides and was surrounded by a curtain wall above a moat about 15ft wide. This has been mostly filled in, but its line can still be traced around the site. The castle is recorded as being abandoned sometime in the early 1600s.

Warkworth Castle

Warkworth Castle stands on a carefully chosen position on the neck of a peninsula, formed by the River Coquet where it flows into the sea. The origins of the castle are generally believed to date back to the time of Ceowulph the Saxon, who had a wooden fortress on the site. But it was during the reign of Henry II that Robert Fitzrichard, son of the Constable of Cheshire, replaced it with a more substantial stone building soon after he had been granted these lands in 1158 for outstanding bravery in battle. His descendants held the castle for almost 200 years, and then it passed by the Royal Charter of Edward III to the powerful Percy family. The king's decision was probably influenced by the idea that such an excellent stronghold in the control of such a powerful family would create a fearsome centre of resistance to the Scots in times of Border trouble. Indeed, for a time the Percys held the important and prestigious position of wardens of the English Middle March.

Warkworth, of course, was the home of the gallant and charismatic Harry Hotspur, the reckless hero of Otterburn and Homildon Hill. It was after the Battle of Homildon Hill that Hotspur became involved in a dispute with the king over who should have the ransom paid for any prisoners. Hotspur, true to his character, rebelled and marched to Shrewsbury to confront the king's army. The

Warkworth Castle.

Percys were defeated and Hotspur was killed; this put an end to any favour that the family held with the Crown, and their estates were forfeited for high treason. However, in 1414 the Percy estates were restored by royal clemency to Hotspur's son who became the 2nd Earl and warden of the English East March. He died in the Wars of the Roses fighting for the royal cause. The Rising of the North, the attempt to restore the Catholic faith, again brought the Percys into conflict with their king and their estates were lost yet again; subsequently the castle was so heavily plundered by Sir John Forster, warden of the English Middle March, that by the time the 8th Earl regained his estates the castle was absolutely ruinous.

It was in such a state that when James I visited in 1617 he declared that it was only the great Percy Lion on the keep that was holding it together.

Woodhouses Bastle, near Rothbury, Northumberland

Woodhouses Bastle is situated to the west of Rothbury near to Holystone Grange. A sympathetic reconstruction provides the opportunity to see how ideally suited to the purpose of defence these fortified houses

Woodhouses Bastle.

were against Border raids. Raiding went on right up to and in some cases beyond the Union of the Crowns in 1603. The walls of these buildings were over 4ft thick and stood to a height of over 20ft with a severely pitched roof, which is now covered with slate but would originally have been thatched with heather. The arched vault, the staircase and a spout over the doorway – useful for pouring molten tar, boiling water or even hot sand over attackers – can all be clearly seen. The doorway arch over the original entrance carries an interesting inscription, WP – BP – 1602, with the letters TAM beneath. These are the initials of William and Bartholomew Potte, members of one of the great Riding surnames, who lived here at that time, although it is believed that the bastle was originally built by Roger Hanginshaws in the mid-1500s.

Jamie Allen, the celebrated Northumbrian Piper, was born at Woodhouses in 1734, and although he did not actually live at the time of the greatest intensity of Border reiving he certainly inherited their character and philosophy. He was of gypsy descent and, we are told, 'he inherited all the cunning and roguery of his race'. He must have been quite a character. His life was one long evasion of the law but his talent on the small pipes earned him great favour with the Duchess of Northumberland. True to character, he soon lost her favour and went off to pursue an irresponsible itinerant life throughout Europe, Asia and Africa. He came home to England in 1803 and was convicted of horse stealing at Durham Assizes and promptly condemned to death. Ostensibly, intervention by the Duchess saw this sentence commuted to transportation. This final journey was not

Woodhouses Bastle.

enforced, possibly due to his poor health, and he spent the final years of his life in the House of Correction in Durham City. Sadly, he died in 1810 on the day before he was granted a pardon by the Prince Regent. His request to be buried near to his home in his native Northumberland was denied, and he was buried in St Nichols' Church Yard, now hidden beneath Durham's busy Market Place. Although it has been said that sometimes, at dusk, the sound of the Northumbrian pipes can be heard on the wind, whistling around Woodhouses Bastle...

The Border Ballads

Apart from official documents like the *Calendar of Border Papers* or the *Calendar of State Papers,* we owe much of what we know about the Reivers' lives to the Border Ballads.

Originally, the ballads would have been sung, and although Sir Walter Scott was heavily criticised for presenting them as poetry they still have a strange and haunting power in this medium. They took the form of epics handed down by word of mouth and were nearly always tragic with occasional flashes of humour. It was an almost inevitable melancholy about the stark realities of life and death that these works so wonderfully portrayed.

A lot of these ballads were rescued from oblivion by Sir Walter Scott, collected on his extensive travels throughout the Borders. It was while he was researching his *Minstrelsey of the Scottish Borders* – a collection of ballads – in 1882 that he got to know James Hogg, who worked as a shepherd on his

Abbotsford, the home of Sir Walter Scott.

Ettrick Kirk. James Hogg is buried in the churchyard.

friend, William Laidlaw's land. It was Hogg, raised in the true Border tradition, who supplied Scott with some of the poetry and ballads that appear, perhaps somewhat modified, in 'the Minstrelsey'. Both writers possessed an astonishing natural narrative sophistication clearly based on their knowledge of Border story-telling traditions.

Perhaps they are best summed up in the words of George Trevellyan, himself a Borderer:

'They were cruel, coarse savages, slaying each other like the beasts of the forest; and yet they were also poets who could express in the grand style the inexorable fate of the individual man and woman, the infinite pity for all cruel things which they none the less perpetually inflicted upon one another. It was not one ballad-maker alone but the whole cut-throat population who felt this magnanimous sorrow and the consoling charms of the highest poetry. The songs on both sides of the Cheviot ridge were handed down by oral tradition among the shepherds, and among the farm-girls who, for centuries, sang them to each other at the milking. If the people had not loved the songs many of the best would have perished. The Border Ballads, for good or evil, express this society and its quality of mind.'

James Hogg monument.